BEYOND

THE

REEDS

BEYOND THE REEDS

Angling forays in search of
species and specimens

John Martin

The Lissanisk Press

First published in 2009 by the Lissanisk Press

Email: themartinsnest@hotmail.com

© John Martin 2009

ISBN: 978-0-9548780-3-0

British Library Cataloguing in Publication Data
A catalogue record for this book is available from the British Library

Printing: Information Press Ltd. (Oxford)

Binding: Green Street Bindery (Oxford)

Cover Design: Eric Holloway, Typecraft (Cheltenham)

Distribution: Coch-y-Bonddu Books Ltd (Machynlleth)

Website: www.anglebooks.com

Telephone 01654—702837

This book has been produced in a limited edition of 300 copies:

Book number: 43

John Martin

Other books by the author:

The Angling Bug (poetry)

It Started With A Perch

Cast A Clever Line

Striking The Inner Chord

Cover picture: River Avon at Eckington (by Lee Martin)

Acknowledgements

This book would not have been possible without my fishing colleagues so I would like to express my gratitude to Richard Fobbester, Andrew Brown, Lord Chick, Paul Mundy, Dave Minchew and the boys in the Barbel Society. A special word is conveyed to my good friend Rawson Bradley for his encouragement and unstinting support, which has taken us across the globe. I would also like to mention Steve Rogers who paved the way for my membership of Smith's Angling Club, allowing me to fish on the lake on Cheltenham Racecourse, which I adore. A further thank you goes out to Jon and Eric at Typecraft and Gilly Bradley who has assisted me with my writing ambitions from the beginning.

*   *   *   *

Introduction

One could be excused for thinking that after a lifetime of fishing I'd be fully conversant with all the things I need to know about the sport, but that's not quite the case. In fact I am continually seeking advice from the specialists and of course, there are always new technological advances that need to be assessed. Fortunately, having already established a solid grounding of all the traditional angling skills, it's a relatively simple task to top up or hone one's knowledge with these new factors. However, the learning process is probably not so easy today for newcomers to our sport as their introduction has more than likely revolved around commercial Carp fisheries and bolt rigs. In my view, this type of initiation is not conducive to achieving the good all-round angling ability that one would have obtained in the past. The modern-day stance may provide instant success, with perhaps larger than average-sized fish, but somehow I feel the new kids on the block are missing out on the real joys of our wonderful pastime. My fear is that we are paying the price of so-called progress here and I can only hope that the old ways don't become lost over the passage of time. For years I have been helping youngsters during their piscatorial pilgrimages on my local stretch of the River Avon, but of late very few young anglers can be found there. It's not as if they've discovered a major disorder such as an infestation of the dreaded Red Signal Crayfish or something similar, and there's still plenty of fish around, so what's the problem? I find this state of affairs very sad and I hope matters improve before too long. Anyway, I'd better get down off the soapbox and try to be more positive about the future. I'm certainly very happy with the kind people who have continued to want to share in my experiences and my approach to angling by purchasing my books. The generous feedback that I have received is not only very much appreciated but also provides the stimulus for me to continue with something that doesn't come easily.

"Book signing" with Paul Morgan — Coch-Y-Bonddu Books

Despite the fact that I could be drawing my old age pension in a few years, I still get a big buzz when planning sorties to track down my target fish. As yet I have not shied away when the going gets tough or resigned myself to the armchair when the weather's turned bad. On the contrary, there are so many new objectives building up on the agenda that it is now becoming nigh on impossible to fit everything in. I must say though that I now prefer shorter stints during the winter months and I'm not so comfortable as I used to be with staying at the waterside for longer than 48 hours. Furthermore, living out of the back of a van on fishing expeditions, which at one time was the story of my life, has now been replaced by more civilised arrangements. Yes, as I approach my twilight years I believe that a little extra time spent on the 'creature comforts' is time well spent. Although in the past these particular issues would never have even been considered, I have come to believe that they not only add to the enjoyment of the sport, but can also improve catch results.

Time to get down to business ....

On the road again — "Now where did I put the fairy liquid?"

Chapter I

Back To The Fenlands –
16th September 2008

Ever since visiting the Burwell Lode at Upware in Cambridgeshire and discovering its big Perch potential, I had been straining at the leash to make a return visit. It was probably the long distance involved, coupled with other fishy commitments, that had prevented me from going back sooner, so I was glad when the little fishery crept back onto the agenda. On my first visit to the place the quarry had been the diminutive Bitterling, which are a rarity in our waters. These little fish are not indigenous to the British Isles and were probably released during the 1960s via an 'aquarium dump', but they have since become established (refer to 'Cast a Clever Line', chapter VI – 'Size Doesn't Always Matter'). In view of the fact that this mission had been specifically planned to catch one of our miniature species, I had been unprepared for the big Perch opportunity that unexpectedly presented itself. Having only been equipped with a boy's whip and ultra-light end tackle, I had been unable to exploit the situation. Since then I had kept the location a secret, until recently when I decided to spill the beans to my old colleague Andrew Brown who had relocated to the area. Andy is a very meticulous and versatile angler who has a very impressive personal best tally to his name and I knew that he would relish the challenge of a new venue, especially if big Perch were involved. For a flavour of his achievements I have selected five of his best fish across a range of species that speak for themselves: Bream 15lb 8ozs, Eel 7lb 4ozs, Barbel 17lb 12ozs (a summer capture!), Nile Perch 98lbs (this was one of eight fish over 90lbs) and Perch 3lb 15ozs. And that's not to forget the 21-inch Toshiba TV caught from a swollen River Severn! Not bad, eh? Anyway, no sooner had I revealed the good news about the promising new Perch venue than he was on the ground in Upware assessing the potential of the water for himself. It was coincidental when he discovered that fishing here was controlled by the Cambridge Fish Preservation and Angling Society, of which he was already a member. I believe that he may have been a little sceptical of my suggestion at first, but soon changed his mind when he found the water teeming with fish that were topping all over the place – better still, there were visible signs of predatory activity as well! Impressed with what he had seen, Andy wasted no time in arranging a visit to test the water with rod and line and it didn't take him long to find the fish. Almost immediately he was getting among some clonkers and, surprisingly, they weren't all Perch. My telephone was hot with the latest news as and when it happened – Andy's excited running commentary of events via his mobile phone was a bit of an eye-opener. To cut a long story short, he had actually caught his first English Rudd over the 2lb mark, along with a large bag of smaller versions. In fact, on the three occasions that he went there he banked no less than ten Perch and six Rudd over 2lbs – a nice result in anyone's book, especially as summer was over. His best Rudd went 2lb 6ozs which was bigger than my best and I was now desperate for a piece of the action as well. Arrangements were therefore made for a joint mission the following week. Andy wanted to be bankside ready for a dawn start so to make things easier it was agreed that I would stop over at his farmhouse the night before our intended visit.

The 133-mile drive to Sawtry Fen was a doddle and, unexpectedly, it was still daylight when I arrived at the main gateway leading to Andy's farm. Situated about a mile along a winding track through countryside, it hadn't been easy to find, but when I did the location was just idyllic. Andy and his wife Virginia have worked tirelessly for 18 months since purchasing the property and now they are reaping the fruits of their labour. The enterprise has blossomed accordingly and their stud farm for Arabian Horses is now considered to be one of the best in Britain. Looking at the number of prestigious awards on display in the trophy room, achieved from both here and the continent, it was obvious that the business is also World renowned. It was fortunate that there was enough daylight left to enable me to look over the place before we had to set about organising tackle and bait in readiness for our early morning venture.

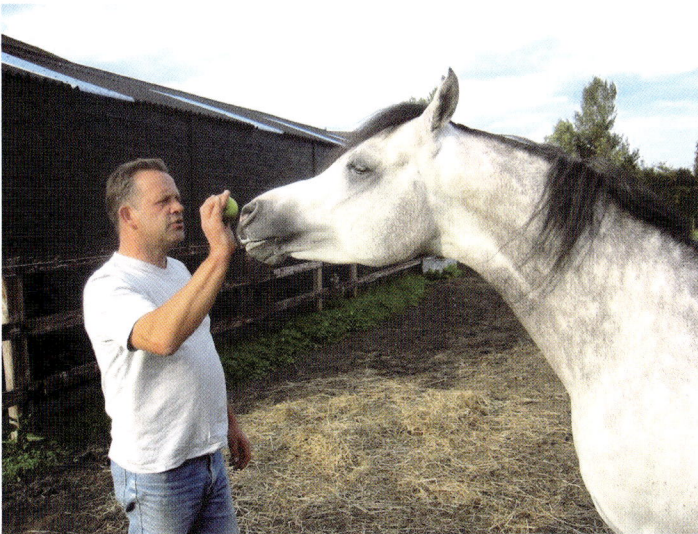

Andy with "Maximus"

I wasn't surprised that there was an autumnal chill in the air when we set out at 4.30am for the 50-minute journey to Upware – our recent mild spell of light south westerly winds had come to an end. The forecast was now for cooler weather with winds coming from an easterly direction which we hoped would not impinge on our summer species assault – this change was just typical of my luck! The question of whether the Rudd would feed as avidly as they had previously was now in the lap of the gods, although we would know soon enough...

We arrived at the sluice gate in Upware a tad before 5.30am. It had been a few years since I'd been there but somehow the place looked different. There appeared to have been some new building work on the far bank and also there was a large stainless steel pillar that hadn't been there before, jutting out vertically from the margins about 20 yards away from the sluice gate. The purpose of this contraption was unknown but we surmised that it had been installed by the water authorities in order to survey the water levels. However, this conclusion was based on pure conjecture so might be wholly inaccurate. Unfortunately the eyesore had been sited directly into the spot where the Bitterling had been thriving and I wondered if they were still present – I'd already made up my mind to check this out as we were departing later that evening.

We set up stall about 400 yards along the lode opposite a line of moored barges and pleasure cruisers. It was important that we didn't crowd each other as we would be trotting floats through our respective pitches, so a gap of about 30 yards was left between us. The first job was to introduce some carefully prepared groundbait which had been plied with plenty of particles including hempseed and miniature pellets. It was imperative to keep the mix light and fluffy so that it would not disturb the fish unduly when it was tossed into the shallowish water. Whilst our number one target had now reverted to Rudd, we didn't want to forego the Perch altogether. To this end, a second rod was made ready with Stripeys in mind, which could be brought into play as and when we felt like it. This meant that, in addition to the groundbait, we would also be spraying plenty of maggots around to attract the prey fish into the target zone as well as the Rudd shoals. The depth of the water was probably in the region of three to four feet in mid-channel, rising to about two feet on the far shelf alongside the barges where the Predators were lurking. It was apparent that the current, flowing from right to left, was heavier than it had been on my previous visit but fortunately this was not to such an extent as to cause us any problems. Within a matter of minutes we had Rudd topping all over the place as they moved in and out of our swims as dawn broke – the prospects looked promising. I was alternating sweetcorn and worms on a size 14 and was taking Rudd after Rudd averaging about 4ozs, although no larger fish came in the first couple of hours. Andy thought the shoals were decidedly more edgy than normal and it was certainly difficult to keep them feeding in the target area for any length of time. Furthermore, it was obvious that the shoals were continually under attack from both Pike and Perch, which was upsetting them somewhat.

The Burwell Lode looking towards the sluice gate

Changing over to the second rod, I lip-hooked a tiny Bream and cast it out towards the barge opposite and within a couple of minutes the two-swan loafer float shot under. I tightened up and struck, connecting with a Jack of about 3lbs, which was duly hooked in the scissors and landed without problem. The small Pike was released 70 yards upstream which I hoped would keep it from homing in on the shoals for at least a couple of hours or so. Whilst I was feeding maggots and a small amount of groundbait with every trot through the swim, it was a complete waste of time using maggots on the hook. No sooner had the float cocked than a small fish, which was inevitably a Rudd or Bream weighing less than an ounce, latched onto the bait. I would have been wasting too much valuable time catching the tiddlers. It was amazing how hectic sport was on this little drain during the mid part of September – the match men would have had a field day. Fishing just over depth seemed to be sorting out the better fish but the remnants of weed growth were causing problems with presentation. However, despite the float constantly dragging under and fragments of weed having to be removed from the bait, persevering with the method was still paying dividends. There was also one other unforeseen setback. For obvious reasons we had specifically chosen to fish opposite the boats that looked devoid of life and had not bargained for the early morning antics of the people in the pleasure cruiser moored between us. One can always expect a certain amount of disturbance from the boating fraternity at a venue like this, but these thoughtless clodhoppers were something else – Michael Flatley and his Riverdance crew had nothing on this lot! With no thought whatsoever for their fellow river-users, this family caused an appalling commotion from the moment they awoke at 8am. As you may appreciate, the catch rate slowed considerably and we were relieved when the happy bunch cast off on a voyage to Cambridge for the rest of the day. Fortunately we were able to re-build the swims and, despite the interruption, by midday both of us had put a lot of nice Rudd up to a pound into the nets, although there had been no two's showing. I'm sure that I'd pricked a few good fish though but they had squirmed off the hook soon after the strike. The Predator rod that had been employed every half hour or so had taken a steady stream of Pike and some medium-sized Perch but it wasn't until late in the afternoon that the larger Perch began coming to the net. During this period it was noticeable how much the flow had reduced, which seemed to bring on the better fish. In fact I took several beauties, with three fish going over the 2lb mark, which incidentally had all taken Rudd livebait. The Perch definitely had a preference for the Rudd while the small Skimmers were seemingly taking the Pike. This was great fishing and it was nice alternating tactics to take some fantastic Rudd to 1lb 5ozs and a net of prime Perch to 2½lbs. Andy had fared similarly and while it was a little disappointing not to have landed a big Rudd, it had still been one of those 'Red Letter' days - and of course there was always tomorrow, as they say.

$$* \qquad * \qquad * \qquad *$$

For any of you out there who fancy a shot at these wonderful fish, the opportunity is open to all of us for the price of a day ticket. You may also be interested to know that since our visit we have been reliably informed of the existence of some huge Rudd (definitely over 3lbs) amongst the enormous shoals of fish that travel throughout the water system. As you may be aware access to venues where Rudd of this calibre can be caught are as rare as rocking horse dung. This is a juicy little venue and I'm sure you won't be disappointed. One point of concern to me though was the fact that the Bitterling had disappeared from their usual place of residence following the decimation of their habitat. I sincerely hope they have just moved on and will subsequently return to their natural environment close to the sluice gate once things have settled down again.

Fenland Perch — "luvvly jubbly"

Chapter II

"Artilleryman" - 25th April 1986

The small band of anglers in the Mercantile and General Sea Angling Club (my former place of work) had gone through the novice stage and were subsequently looking for some 'big boys' fishing. They had sampled the delights of Dogfish and Rays inshore and now wanted to visit some deep-water wrecks to try for some heavyweights. We decided to do it properly by chartering 'Artilleryman II', skippered out of the Port of Plymouth by the famous Geordie Dickson – surely he would be able to find some rod benders for us! There were four in our party, joining another couple of lads from Torrington to make up a crew of six. This number was ideal because it would mean there would be ample room to fish when we finally arrived at the shipwrecks lying three hours steam away in the English Channel. The journey along the M5 took a tad over two hours during the early morning, which was good going seeing as we covered 170 miles. The fast run ensured that we had enough time for a hearty 'full English' and some piping hot tea before we set out on our adventure. A greasy breakfast was par for the course on our trips, although some of us did come to regret it later, especially when the sea was lumpy. Approaching the marina I was reminded of a unique piece of local history that overlooks the sea just along the way at Plymouth Hoe. I have always been fascinated by our lighthouses and in particular their construction, and here was a fine example for all to see. The monument in question was 'Smeaton's Tower' which was a former lighthouse built on the Eddystone Reef in Plymouth Sound by John Smeaton and his team of masons in 1759. In fact this wonderful construction would still have been on the reef today had it not been for the rock on which it stood becoming unstable due to erosion. This meant that Smeaton's Tower had to be replaced by a new lighthouse which was built on an adjacent rock. However, so as not to lose an important part of our heritage, the whole thing was painstakingly dismantled, transported and re-erected where it stands today on Plymouth Hoe – now there's a fine example of English ingenuity for you!

Smeaton's Tower on Plymouth Hoe

Anyway, reverting back to the mission... all arrangements went like clockwork and we set out on schedule towards Geordie's chosen marks. 'Artilleryman' was a fast boat and it didn't seem long before the sight of land was lost altogether. Unbeknown to me at the time, the boat's smooth steering system was dependent on the passengers remaining still so I was taken aback when Geordie cut engines and came out of his cabin to have a word with me. Apparently I had been flitting from pillar to post and in the process was upsetting the course that Geordie had set. I'd heard through the sea angling grapevine that he was a tough character with a reputation for being a strong disciplinarian and I now had first hand experience of it! I learned later that Geordie, who was born in 1936, had enlisted in the Royal Artillery as a boy entrant at the age of 16, which is how the boat got its name. Albeit, as far as skippers go, they didn't come much better than Geordie. I would guess that we had reached about half way to the first wreck mark when Geordie had to make a second unscheduled stop. All of a sudden there had been an almighty thud which was heard above the noise of the powerful engines as we sped through the waves. The impact with the foreign object, which as far as I was concerned could have been the size of a grand piano, was severe and certainly shook us up a little. As 'Artilleryman' bobbed about in the swell, we scoured around to see if we could locate the piece of offending flotsam but there was nothing to be seen – it appeared that the boat's velocity had left it well behind us by the time we had actually stopped. Everybody was looking a bit sheepish and I'm sure we were all thinking about donning the life-jackets, expecting the sea to start billowing up through the deck at any moment. Fortunately Geordie carried out a quick damage assessment and, finding that we hadn't been holed or disabled, we were able to continue on our way. Phew - for a moment it looked like an air-sea rescue job! Anyway it appeared that this charter was becoming one of those eventful affairs. After our little crisis, most of the chaps took the sensible decision to grab some shut-eye during the rest of the steam. However, as always, I was unable to follow suit because I was still buzzing with excitement at the prospect of what might be coming next.

As we neared the first wreck location, the lads became a bit restless and began jockeying for position in readiness to drop their lines. We had all set up with similar end tackle consisting of a 15 foot flowing trace (in my case, 18lb breaking strain monofilament), which was finished off with a large 'Redgill'. Geordie had suggested that we alternate both black and orange gills as these had been taking the majority of fish during his recent forays. After a few passes, Geordie found his path across the wreck and manoeuvred the boat into position accordingly for the first drift. We all waited eagerly for his command to lower away the end tackle to the sea floor as he watched the outline of the wreck approaching on his electronic display. 'Okay boys, down you go' and on cue we all plunged our leads into the blue at the same time – no-one wanted to be last as this could mean missing out on the action. The leads seemed to be slipping away through the depths for an eternity - we were certainly fishing in deep water. Only one fish was taken on the first drift, which was a nice sized Pollack that must have been close to 10lbs. Subsequent drifts produced a whole lot more of the same, with everybody taking a few fish before the hook-ups began to wane. My best fish weighed in at 12¾lbs, which happened to be a personal best Pollack and I was well happy. After about an hour of hectic sport, Geordie decided to move on to another wreck location, less than half hours steam away.

There was just enough time for a cup of tea before we had to get down to business again and it was nice to see that the rest of the crew were 'chipper' after sampling the delights of the first fish sanctuary – the boys were certainly enjoying this charter. As before, the adrenalin began to flow when Geordie's navigational co-ordinates showed that wreck number two was close at hand. He reduced speed to a mere tick-over and once again found his line of approach. It never ceases to amaze me how a skipper can suddenly bring his boat to a virtual standstill at the precise location of a shipwreck in the middle of a vast sea. Having travelled for hours upon end in an unchanging environment, I always look around instinctively for some kind of clue but invariably there are no signs or markers as to what lies beneath. On each occasion the distant horizon shows the same old picture of mile upon mile of open sea, with no hint of the fact that a ship's grave lies below – talk about trying to find a needle in a haystack! Anyway, as the fishing commenced at the second wreck, the sport continued as it had done before, with a stream of hefty Pollack coming aboard at regular intervals. In fact I was reeling in a nine-pounder when I began experiencing problems with my Mitchell 624. I was unable to put my finger on exactly what was wrong with it, but retrieving the lure was definitely proving more difficult. The usual smooth retrieve had been lost which was very frustrating, not only from the fishing point of view but because, as far as I could see there was nothing at fault with the multiplier. In practice it meant that the lure's action as it was drawn up from the wreck was slightly out of sync, which must have been off-putting to the fish. They must have sensed some sort of abnormality because from then on I caught no further fish while everybody else continued to catch big-time. There was hardly any spare time between drifts and my only focus was to get the Redgill back to the bottom as soon as Geordie gave the word to fish. Of course I should have taken time out to resolve the problem rather than continuing to fish with a defective reel. In fact it wasn't until I returned home that I discovered a tiny screw was missing from the outer casing of the reel, which in effect had unbalanced the spool's rotation. The timing of this minor catastrophe - which I still think about today - couldn't have been worse because during the last hour

Geordie managed to put us over a section of the wreck which must have been occupied by a shoal of specimen Coalfish. Every angler on board – apart from myself that is – started to connect with these wonderful fish, which put up a terrific battle. During the relatively short spell, a steady stream of them were brought up from the depths to the surface where they floundered on the tide. These huge white-bellied fish, held in the blue swell before being brought on board, made an awesome sight. In all about eight of these superb fish were caught, of which a good percentage weighed in excess of 20lbs. What a coup this had been and I just wished that I had seen some of the action for myself. By the time the fishing was over the hold was brimming with prime Pollack and Coalfish. The day had certainly been a memorable one for me despite the disappointment of not getting amongst the Coalies.

You can appreciate that I had to take a lot of stick on the way back to port from the other lads who had scored so dramatically when it mattered. Here was I, the so-called expert, being shown the way by the beginners, who had literally cleaned up with the big Coalies! At the time I hadn't dared to make the excuse of a faulty reel being the reason for my poor performance as that would have sounded like a bad bout of sour grapes. I have thought long and hard about the situation since that day and realise how important the presentation of a Redgill must be. Previously I had assumed that the predatory wreck lurkers would have attacked anything thrown in their direction but in practice this is definitely not the case. It would appear that the movement of artificial Eels should closely resemble that of the predator's natural prey in every way possible in order to induce a take. Anyway, during the long steam home, Geordie got in touch with the angling press who sent a correspondent to meet us at the quay for the story and some photographs. It was a pity that the pictures of these magnificent fish couldn't have been taken at the time of their capture when they were simply bristling in their natural livery. After a few hours in the hold, during which time rigor mortis sets in, the images can never be as enthralling. Nevertheless, the man from the press met us as arranged and the proud captors lined up with their Coalfish haul for a group photograph. From memory I believe the article was shown in the following month's issue of 'Sea Angler' and was also featured in the 'Angler's Mail' – bravo, chaps!

*   *   *   *

KED STONE

the better codling.

Dymchurch Bay dinghy anglers found up to 60 dabs at a session on flowing traces. **Dungeness** also a good flattie bet, the best falling to black lug. Small codling landed. **Dengemarsh** turned up flounders to 1½ lb and numerous codling.

Bob Fisher's **Ramsgate** boat "Halloday", took some good skate and cod. Richard Traster took a 20 lb cod and a 13 lb ray! Three other anglers on the boat each took a 20 lb cod.

Ramsgate's "Pauline" took 24 skate to 14 lb. The odd mackerel and the first garfish showing off Thanet and dabs shoaling close to shore. Other Ramsgate boats taking rays from the Goodwin Sands together with dogfish.

Plenty of codling on inshore marks, most fish 1-2 lb. Dabs from the **Margate** area with small codling. Thornback ray on the Margate Sands and also from the Woolpack off **Reculver** and the Pan Sands off **Herne Bay**. The first bass also caught on the Sands with small codling and flatties from inshore marks.

Peeler crab available throughout the area and essential for the codling on the chalk ledges in the North Foreland area. Good silver eels from boats and North Kent beaches.

Ramsgate Harbour, Marina Beach and **Western Undercliff** worth a visit with small codling dominating catches.

BIG PLAICE FOR PIER ANGLERS

SOME big plaice are making the headlines along the South Coast with two five-pounders taken from pier marks.

Clive Smedley landed a 5 lb fish at Hastings Pier while Eastbourne Pier turned up a specimen of 5½ lb.

Mark Hall of the Pevensey Bay Aqua Club caught a 4½ lb plaice from the beach at Normans Bay to help him into second place during a club competition.

● GRAHAM HOOPER, Paul Lawrence, Rawson Bradley, and Richard Sunman of Cheltenham had a field day with coalfish at a wreck lying south of Plymouth located by Geordie Dickson skipper of "Artilleryman II." All their fish scaled between 15 and 21 lb and were taken on black artificials offered on flowing traces.

Other catches during the match included flounders, small codling and eels.

Bexhill beaches for dabs, flounders and the odd bass; best bait black lugworm. **Langney Point** best at night for codling; dabs and some plaice taken during the day.

Boats off **Eastbourne** and **Newhaven** found a few spurdogs. Cod and conger from wrecks. **Brighton** beaches yielded flounders and plaice from Holland Road to white and red ragworm.

Eastney, Southsea and **Hayling Island** beaches produced flounders and a few plaice. Plenty of school bass with up to 25 fish a session reported, but most are small and should go back. One angler took seven up to 4½ lb from **Southampton Water** on ragworm.

Charter boats in the area taking plenty of smoothhound, dogfish, conger and rays. The first mackerel

appearing on the wrecks so big fish should be around soon.

Sport off **Littlehampton** good with skippers reporting heavy catches of spurs to 15 lb. Bags made up of rays, conger, dogfish, pout and large Channel whiting. Increasing numbers of mackerel on feathers. Lots of pollack taken on the drift with ling and conger from the bottom. First bass from inshore marks.

Isle of Wight anglers found a lot of lesser-spotted dogfish on shore marks with the best areas Chale to Atherfield, Ryde Pier and Sandown Bay. A lot of garfish also taken from Sandown Bay and Shanklin Pier.

Pollack reported from Shanklin and Sandown Piers, also plaice, flounders and dabs.

Boat angling over the Needles area good with sizeable thornback rays, dogfish and large pouting.

ANGLER'S MAIL Week-ending May 17, 1986   29

A young Rawson Bradley, third from the left, with a brace of twenty-pounders!

Chapter III

Snake Hunt - July 2008

Despite having had an exchange of correspondence regarding Eel tactics and rigs with the legendary John Sidley during his 'Put Eels Back' campaign in the late 1970s, I have never actually got around to any serious assault on Anguilla anguilla. The reason for this omission from my angling programme is unclear but is probably because I mistakenly felt that there were better targets to be had at the time. However, during latter years my desire to catch a big Eel intensified and I therefore began to actively search out local venues that I felt had the necessary potential to achieve this goal. I had set my sights on a couple of pools that appeared to have the right credentials for producing some decent Snakes, although these very private wildlife havens seemed to be a little out of reach. Anyway, I decided to take the step of writing to the landowners to explain my quest and, lo and behold, I received permission to fish for 24 hour stints on both pools – it just goes to show that a courteous approach like this can pay real dividends!

The next important decision was tackle and bait. There was much to consider here because, in my limited experience of the species, these fish can be extremely wily and have a habit of dropping a bait at the slightest resistance. I can perceive some of you scoffing at this remark because small Eels have the annoying habit of gorging baits without hesitation. However, I can assure you that it's a different story as far as big Eels and big baits are concerned. I thought that Zander were bad enough when it came to dropping baits but in practice I have found that Eels are even more prone to this tendency. Looking back, I can only remember making a few serious attempts at jumbo Eels, mostly during times of boredom when my main quarry had been reluctant to feed. Using dead baits I've taken a few fish above 2lbs, mainly from still waters, but even these modestly-sized fish have required much guile and patience – slippery customers indeed! As a general rule of thumb, I have found that bites have been difficult to hit because the timing of the strike always seems to have an element of guesswork involved in it. The problem had been deciding on whether a fish had actually taken a bait or was just grabbing hold of a section of it before running for cover. In the majority of instances the Eels had charged off at speed, which had meant employing an open spool policy in order to have any chance of making a connection with them. In hindsight, a better ploy would have been to reduce the size of the bait which, in theory, would have allowed an earlier strike. However, in saying that, smaller baits are more than likely going to attract 'bootlaces', which are probably a worse problem – you can't win! Taking everything into consideration, my tackle preference was a simple running leger rig in conjunction with a 2oz lead to hold things in position. Hook size would be a size 4 attached to a two-foot length of 15lb breaking strain braided link, and main line would be my trusty Maxima in a 10lb strain. Crucially, I would also employ an improvised bobbin made from a 10 inch section of wire bent over at the centre to hang on the line. This simple device has just enough weight to hold position when pulled to the floor and yet drops off on the strike, thus avoiding any tangling problems. With this facility the option to use either an open or closed bale arm would still be at my disposal. If an open spool approach was to come into play, I would tuck a loop of the line under an elastic band attached to the butt of the rod instead. My bait was to consist of Lobworms, Dendrobaena Worms, half sections of fresh Roach and Rudd deadbaits, and Prawns.

Black Swan Pool - 10th July 2008

The first choice venue was a beautifully landscaped pool in the village of Beckford in Worcestershire. According to the owner, the lake is nameless so I've taken it upon myself to call it Black Swan Pool due to the fact that when I first discovered it in 1989 it was home to a lone Black Swan – sentimental old fool! The Swan is long gone but now the place is bristling with a multitude of waterfowl, including a large flock of Geese. I would certainly have to make a softly, softly approach to ensure that I caused minimum disturbance to both birds and their environment at the appropriate time. I was aware that the brown coloured waters held a good head of Carp but could only guess that the venue also contained an Eel population. It was an educated guess though as the Carrant Brook flows in close proximity to the pool, which should have provided the relevant means for habitation. During the week prior to my intended bout of fishing, I took the liberty of recce-ing the pool in order to find a suitable spot to try my luck. As it turned out, there were strangely very few places available to set up stall despite the lake covering several acres. Most of the banks were either very marshy, overgrown with trees and bushes or had the remnants of tree roots extending into the margins. However, I did manage to find a glorious spot which had a suitable depth and enough open water to be able to land a big Eel should one come my way. Furthermore, I could see plenty of small fish rising which would hopefully mean that I could obtain some silver fish for bait without too much trouble – the butterflies in my stomach were now stirring with anticipation!

Settled in for the night ahead

There was a fresh south-westerly airstream, the sky was overcast and atmospheric pressure was on the low side, registering 999mb, when I slotted into my chosen patch. I had arrived at noon at the picturesque pool to begin my Eel campaign and it was looking good for one of those mild and dark nights that I love. Having assembled my equipment and got myself comfortable, the first task was to secure some livebait. With light float tackle I had no trouble in accumulating half a dozen small Roach and Rudd which were going to be ample for a night's stint. The fish were placed in my handy livebait net which incorporated a pull string top to prevent the fish escaping when the net was submerged in the margins. The 'Catfish boys' had introduced me to these nets, which enable fish to be extracted when needed without too much fuss. Cor blimey, I hope no-one was watching or they'd be calling me a 'tackle tart' next – better move on! Next item on the agenda was the introduction of some attractor consisting of chopped sections of fish, Dendrobaena Worms duly scissored, and some Prawns for good measure mixed with brown crumb. The concoction was balled in randomly across the general target area in order to lay down a scent trail which would hopefully stimulate the Eels into a feeding frenzy – famous last words!

It was 3pm when I made my first casts. I had chosen to use a large bunch of Lobworms on both rods - to test the water as they say. Initially I opted to fish with closed spools, hoping to connect by the time the bobbin had travelled about four feet to the rod butt. This tactic was an unknown quantity so only time would tell if it was good policy. Within all of 30 seconds of the baits settling, the left hand rod's bobbin was sailing to the butt at a rate of knots and I struck into my first fish. I hadn't expected action quite so quickly and, although the rod had a healthy bend on it, I wasn't convinced it was an Eel that had taken the bait. The culprit had kited to the right of my position and I waited anxiously to get a glimpse of the thing that felt like a dead weight at the end of the line. Disappointingly, it was a Mirror Carp of about 4lb that came to the surface in front of me – oh dear, Lobworms were a classic bait for Eels but on this occasion they would have to be disregarded in favour of some deadbait in order to deter the Carp. The last thing I needed was to waste my precious time using a bait that was going to attract something other than the target fish.

Both rods were rebaited accordingly, one with the head end of a Roach and the other, using a baiting needle, with the tail section. In view of their nocturnal feeding habits, I wasn't expecting any activity from the Eels until dusk and so was pleasantly surprised when, at 7pm, the alarm on the right hand rod jogged me back to reality. Seemingly, I timed the strike perfectly and connected with another rod bender which veered off at speed before heading back towards the margins on the right of my position. It felt like a good fish but, despite the pressure applied, I was unable to change the route it was taking. The fish continued on its bankward course and inevitably got dangerously close to some Willow Tree roots, when I had to tighten the clutch down in order to try to gain line. It was a last resort and unfortunately the heavy sidestrain pressure to avoid the hazard proved too much and the hook pulled prematurely – it was back to the drawing board.... The sky was darkening early in view of the cloud cover and the Bats seemed to be everywhere. This was Eel time and I was confident that it wouldn't be too long before I bagged one. In order to avoid the possibility of lines tangling when a fish was hooked during the night, I decided to reel in one of the rods, the one with the Roach tail. The coast was now clear and I settled down to await developments. The resident rodent population kept me amused with their comings and goings while I waited for some Eel action. They could obviously smell my savoury snacks which I had to protect as their brazen attempts to steal them became bolder. Anyway, it was 9.25pm when the mini-micron began to sound out the good news that something had intercepted my half dead bait. Without going through the drama again, it was in fact another Mirror Carp of about 5lbs that came to the net and I was astounded to find that the beast had taken the head and half the body of a Roach, which severely jeopardised my Eel ambitions. I suddenly found myself in a quandary as to what to do next; the carnivorous Carp had scuppered my plans. I concluded that the only course of action left open to me was to use livebait and so I hooked a six-inch Rudd through both lips and re-cast. I hadn't experienced this behaviour from Carp before, although I had heard that they can sometimes have predatory tendencies. It wasn't as if I'd used a small bait either, which might have given reason for a hungry Carp to intercept the offering. No, I was bemused by the incident and a little concerned that my aspirations for success at this captivating pool weren't looking quite so straightforward.

All was quiet except for the commotion caused by the Geese that seemed to be forever entering and exiting the pool via the island. The temperature had dropped by now and I could barely see my hand in front of my face. Surprisingly, the livebait hadn't been active enough to give me any false bites – I had been expecting the bobbin to jump about a bit as the tethered fish buffeted at the end of the line. There was no activity for a couple of hours and then – bingo! - the alarm was suddenly bleeping again. I waited for all of two seconds for the bobbin to climb to the butt before striking successfully. There was a satisfying response and the rod buckled and thumped as the fish tried to make its escape. I wanted to dictate the battle from the beginning so once again I played the fish hard to prevent it getting close to snags. Bullying fish in this manner was not my usual approach but, in the circumstances, I felt it was the best policy. Within a minute the power of the tackle had brought the fish into the open water in front of me and I waited eagerly to catch a glimpse of it in the beam of my head torch. Soon enough the fish was in netting range but my heart sank when the golden flanks of another Mirror Carp, again about 5lbs, was illuminated in the light. This strange occurrence just wasn't in the script and somehow I felt cheated by the outcome. Using a livebait had been my last throw of the dice and I had no alternative strategy to fall back upon. It was time to pack up and head for home.

The idea of predatory Carp spoiling my Eel campaign was as much baffling as it was disappointing. I suppose that the Rudd may have already been dead by the time the Carp had discovered it but even if this had been the case it was still far from their normal habits. On reflection, I believe that this unusual behaviour had been stimulated by the chopped fish that had been introduced as groundbait at the beginning of the session. Anyway, it was now over to the other venue on my list.

Beggarboys Pool - 17th July 2008

Having only seen this pool from some distance a couple of years prior to obtaining permission to fish, I needed to have a closer look in advance of any serious fishing attempt. There was no vehicular access to the place and so an inspection was going to mean a very pleasurable hike across the western slopes of Bredon Hill. The pool was tucked away in the confines of a small nature reserve that was very secluded indeed and I was keeping my fingers crossed that I would remember how to get there.

It was a perfect summer's day when I set out on my reconnaissance mission, starting from the little Edward VII letter box set into a Cotswold stone wall in the village of Upper Westmancote. From here I was able to pick up the path towards Bredons Norton that I had used on my previous visit – so far so good. I was on my way so now it was a case of following my instincts and hoping for the best. The trek took me well off the beaten track and I was mighty glad that the ground was dry. Nevertheless, it was still a hard slog and I kept thinking that my stamina levels were going to be put to the test when I returned next time fully laden with the kit. On the day I was surprised that I hadn't seen the usual Fallow Deer but to make up for it there were Rabbits galore and plenty of wheeling Buzzards to admire. During the hike across scores of acres of farmland, I came to the conclusion that the 'in crop' must have been 'Horse Beans' because every field that I could see stretching into the distance seemed to be full of them – surely there couldn't be a market for that lot! By now I had travelled a fair way and I was beginning to wonder whether I had taken a wrong turn when I stumbled on the little gate and plaque which proclaimed that I had arrived at Beggarboys – wonders will never cease!

A little wildlife haven tucked away amid Bredon Hill

I popped over the gate and followed the path that meandered into a green maze which didn't appear to have experienced any human intervention for years. Looking over the layout of the natural wildlife habitat, there was an area of Willow coppice, extensive beds of sedge, two small glades and woodland at the far end of the pool. It was very picturesque although it was plainly evident that access for fishing was going to be more than problematical. In order to get closer to the banks of the pool, I firstly had to plough through a marshy area full of Common Rush and Water Mint – I should have brought the waders! The intoxicating scent of the crushed mint was lovely but at the same time the going was difficult for an old man. Having reached the margins, I then had to fight my way painstakingly through a tangled mass of brambles and the like along the steep sloping banks towards the deeper end of the pool. It must have taken me a good 20 minutes to make 20 yards and when I arrived at the only viable place for casting a line, discovered that the whole lake was covered with a thick layer of blanket weed lying a foot or so below the surface. Without a great deal of tree lopping and weed dragging, which would have been totally unacceptable in that secret place, the Eel campaign was obviously a non-starter – c'est la vie! It was just as well that I had taken along a light float outfit and some maggots in order to determine whether I could catch livebait on site, as this was some compensation for my efforts. There were plenty of fish rising and it didn't take long to accumulate a nice bag of prime Roach up to 4ozs. Whilst I was a little bit disappointed at not being able to have a crack at the Eels, the Roach had at least been one consoling factor.

Apparently, in the days of yore, this little patch of ground was witness to the hanging of two young beggars who had been caught stealing and they say that the place has been haunted ever since. In hindsight, the prospect of spending a night at this remote location wasn't something I would have relished. These unforeseen circumstances had brought the snake hunt to a premature end and I had to quickly come up with an alternative venue if I was to continue with my quest. My local club water on Cheltenham National Hunt Racecourse was certainly purported to hold some Pythons but I had been reluctant to try for them there in view of the strictly-enforced barbless hook and no night-fishing regulations. However, in light of recent developments, it was now necessary to forget my reservations and get on with the task ahead.

Cheltenham Racecourse Pool - 28th July 2008

This is one of the most scenic, comfortable and interesting fisheries that one could wish for. Smiths' Angling Club have worked wonders developing the pool to provide the membership with consistent sport from a variety of species that are fast growing to specimen proportions. It's gratifying to know that they haven't gone down the 'Stocky Carp' route that most fisheries sadly follow today. The current fish population includes Tench, Roach, Rudd, Perch, Crucian Carp, Brown Goldfish, Chub, Grass Carp, a smattering of large King Carp and, of course, Eels. I now look upon the place as my special retreat where I am completely at home doing what I love doing. It never seems to get too busy and even when the fish aren't biting there are magnificent views across the racecourse to savour. Rolling green uplands backed up by nigh on 1,000 feet of Cotswold escarpment known as 'Cleeve Cloud' creates a scintillating picture. Apart from the scenic attraction, there is also an abundance of bird life including a high number of Grey Herons that seem to be tamer than normal. They can be observed at close quarters stalking their prey amongst the water lilies, along with a solitary Little Egret that seems to have set up residence there. It's certainly nice for me to have such a pleasurable place on my doorstep in which to cast a line and I'm glad that I was fortunate enough to obtain membership, which is by invitation only. In fact I was honoured to have been introduced to the club by one of our local angling personalities, Ron Cooper, who pioneered big Barbel fishing on the lower reaches of the River Severn during the 1990s – cheers Ron!

I arrived at the fishery gates at about noon and was expecting to remain on the fishery until the last possible moment before darkness set in at about 9pm. I chose a spot with a good expanse of water lilies close by rather than one of open water because I felt that the Eels would be holed up there during the daylight hours. To entice them out, I fired a few King Prawns into the target zone before baiting my hook carefully with a Worm ball! Firstly, two large Lobworms were impaled and pulled over the eye of the hook onto the braided hook link before finishing things off with three more Dendrobaenas and a Prawn to hold everything in place. Wow, it was a big bait and I couldn't wait to see if there were going to be any takers. After about 45 minutes I noticed that the line between the rod tip and the surface of the lake twitched forwards and then tightened. Within seconds of this initial movement, I was following the bobbin's path towards the rod before striking into my first Eel. One normally has an inkling when an Eel is hooked because of the repetitive whirling motion that transmits along the line to the rod tip. This circumstance occurs as the fish squirms its body into a ball then proceeds to pull its head backwards through its muscular coils to create the maximum resistance as the angler attempts to haul it through the water. The plucky Eel put a nice bend in the rod although the relatively heavy tackle soon had it beaten and I was able to net it without problem. This fish turned out to be a very pleasing 2lbs plus but, whilst it had been a good start to the campaign, the Eel was not quite what I had been hoping for. Fortunately, the barbless hook had held but I was still far from comfortable fishing for such grand 'contortionists' without the reassurance of that microscopic spur which is usually so dependable. Let's face it, a dream could be dashed on such a triviality. I must say there are times when I am almost confident using barbless hooks but this occasion wasn't one of them!

Once again I hooked up the worms fastidiously to ensure that the presentation would be irresistible to any resident Eel before casting out just beyond the lily pads about 25 yards away from my position. As I sat and soaked up the ambience, patches of needle-sized bubbles were fizzing here and there as the bottom feeders went about their business – oh boy, this was an idyllic place to fish! A cockle on a size 10 would have produced an instant result had Tench and Crucians been on the agenda. In fact I had to wait a further hour before there was another pull that took the indicator to within a foot of the rod but that's as far as it went – my suspicion was that the wily creature had felt something untoward and quickly jettisoned the bait. I remained poised for the next 10 minutes in case the culprit gave me a second chance, but nothing transpired. I decided to reel in, only to discover that the hook had been cleaned. This was slightly irritating because I was sure that a barbed hook would not have given up the juicy offering quite so easily. My initial reservations had been awakened again, although there was nothing further I could do but carry on regardless.

The next fish came at tea-time, a surprise Tench that weighed in at 6lb 11ozs. Catching this fish put a whole new perspective on the fishing as these olive-coloured warriors were now approaching double figure weights here and I had the distinct feeling that I might just get lucky. Nevertheless, all was quiet for the next couple of hours before the bobbin was rising again. This fish turned out to be another Eel and a better one at that, going a tad under 3lbs – that was more like it, although I was still hoping for a bit more. Fishing in this fashion made a change from the norm and my expectations were on a high. The chances of catching a specimen fish were always on the cards in view of the size of the bait that I was using – it was hardly going to be sucked in by a tiddler.

At 8.40pm another screaming run occurred and I immediately connected with something much more substantial. A solid force was whirling away at the end of the line which had bent my through-action rod over to its maximum. I was reluctant to ease the pressure because I didn't want to give the Eel any headway whatsoever for fear of it getting into snags. My heart began to race as I realised that this was the biggie I had been hoping for. Gradually I pumped the beast shorewards, managing to avoid the large bed of water lilies to my left. I was winning the battle but it required plenty of brute force and concentration to overcome its uncanny strength and erratic plunges for freedom. More heavy pressure began to pay dividends and the fish soon came within a few yards of netting range. It was still fighting doggedly to hold its position when all of a sudden it broke surface and I nearly had a heart attack. It was the biggest Eel I'd ever clapped eyes on – the girth of the thing was immense! Sadly my euphoria was short-lived. In fact, I was actually reaching out with the net when disaster struck – the damned hook had pulled free as the angry eel writhed and twisted in a flurry of spray tantalisingly close to the rim of the 42-inch frame of the net. It was a shattering blow and I cursed audibly as my deep frustration immediately hit home. Stone the crows, I was within seconds of landing the fish of a lifetime and I couldn't help thinking that this unfortunate loss could have been avoided had an appropriate hook been employed. Of course I was bitterly disappointed but at the same time I did wholeheartedly accept that this fishery was run for the match and pleasure angler and not for the likes of myself who was taking time out to try for a specimen. I can't stress this point enough, it's just how the cookie crumbles sometimes – you win some, you lose some!

On reflection it's difficult to describe how gutted I actually felt. For several weeks afterwards the scene was replayed in my mind and I was unable to shake from my head the image of the Python being lost at the critical moment. It truly was a dire loss but, make no bones about it, I will catch that Eel one day. The memory will continue to plague me until such time that I do manage to slip my net under it – at least I now know the venue to satisfy this burning ambition. For this year however time had run out for the Eel quest and so a new venture would have to be put on hold until next summer. The rivers were now beckoning and my attention would soon be turning to the Princely Barbus.

*   *   *   *

My consolation prize but a nice fish all the same

Chapter IV

Wrasse City – 29ᵗʰ May 2008

The prospect of fishing at this prolific mark, which I had nicknamed Wrasse City, was mouth-watering to say the least and I couldn't wait to drop a line into the hotspot. I had fished the mark at Porthoustock, on Cornwall's southern coast, on previous occasions and I was more than confident of seeing plenty of action when the tide reached its pinnacle. Porthoustock is one of those little hamlets on the Lizard Peninsula that has largely remained unspoiled, probably due to the fact that access to the place is relatively difficult. Both approach roads down to the village and the beach can be a little nerve-racking for the faint-hearted motorist, especially during inclement weather. Not only are these thoroughfares extremely narrow but they incorporate hairpin bends and a one-in-four gradient. Nevertheless, the hazardous journey is worth every bead of nervous sweat and flutter in the lower regions as the sport to be had there can be second to none. The precise location of the 'city mark' is easy to find as it lies adjacent to an obsolete storage silo which used to house crushed quarry stone. It wasn't so long ago that ships were brought alongside this building to have their holds filled with the stuff ready for onwards transportation to far and beyond. Despite being a somewhat ugly feature in the naturally rugged landscape, it does provide a feel for how things were. Access to this relatively deep water mark is via a narrow concrete gantry that stretches around three sides of the silo. The seabed here is rocky and there is plenty of kelp to attract Ballans, Corkwings, Goldsinny and even Rock Cook Wrasse, although I don't believe that it is quite deep enough for Cuckoos – I haven't caught one yet anyway. I love fishing for Wrasse as they are normally very obliging, they fight like demons and there are numerous baits readily available that can be utilised. Crabs are arguably the best bait for Wrasse but, for ease, I generally use both raw and cooked Prawns, Cockles and Ragworms. On this occasion I had opted for cooked Prawns which were impaled onto a blued Kamasan Crab hook size 4 (pattern number B900c). These hooks have short shanks and are extremely sharp and so are ideal for baiting with soft shellfish like Prawns. My rod had already been assembled with a running leger rig although, in hindsight, I'd have preferred a paternoster arrangement, for two reasons. Firstly, Wrasse have a tendency to swallow a bait quickly which can sometimes mean deep hooking. In my experience bites can be detected slightly quicker on a paternoster set-up where the hook snoods are generally shorter. Secondly, fishing directly below my position would have meant a bait fluttering enticingly just above the rocky bottom rather than being down amongst the debris. However, for the sake of not wasting precious time, I decided to stick with the standard running tackle and would take heed to strike at the earliest indication to try and avoid the fish gorging the bait.

Looking down towards the silo at Porthoustock

It was reaching the top of the tide when I lowered the succulent bait down the edge of the wall towards the target area, which was a tiny clear patch between weeds and boulders. The line was quickly tightened up as the sinker hit bottom so I would be in a position to register any bites as soon as they occurred. In fact there was no waiting necessary at all as the rod folded immediately without warning as a Ballan charged off to seek sanctuary in the rocky terrain below. The power of the fish was such that the reel began to concede line, allowing it to get into the kelp, which is normally fatal. My 10lb breaking strain hook link wouldn't have taken too much abrasion so I had to take care not to overdo it trying to get the fish moving again. All had gone solid so I slackened the line for a few seconds before striking again, which fortunately brought the Wrasse back into open water. This little dodge did the trick and after a couple more lunges the beautifully-marked fish surfaced ready for the net. But there was one problem – I hadn't brought one! There wasn't any need to worry though as it was just a matter of working the fish back to the grey pebbled beach for the landing. A few minutes later the beaten fish was floundering on the surface just out of reach, so I used the action of the waves to help bring it onto the shingle shore where it could be plucked from the surf. By good luck it had been lip hooked and I didn't have to delve into those dreaded jaws that in some respects resemble those of Sharks. I estimated the weight of the Ballan to be about 3lbs before getting a quick photograph and releasing it back into the shelving waters. Without further ado I clambered back onto the concrete apron and edged my way around to the deep water section at the front end of the silo again. Oh boy, was I enjoying myself already and I still had the best part of an hour's fishing left before attention would have to be switched to normal family holiday commitments. Two juicy Prawns were hooked up this time hopefully with the larger fish in mind that provide the heart-racing action loved by all anglers. My 2lb test curve Pike rod was just the tool for the job and it was only a matter of seconds after the bait hitting the bottom that I was into another rod-bender. This fish veered left and once again was able to battle its way into the labyrinth of wrack and rock that paved the seabed there. Despite applying maximum pressure I was unable to prevent the fish going to ground and this time there was nothing I could do to prise it out from its refuge – I had to pull for a break and re-tackle.

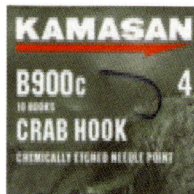

Wrassing on the silo - a Ballan heads for cover
in the rocky terrain below

My attention was drawn to a group of divers who had been preparing their gear on the beach and were now about to enter the sea in their distinctive black and fluorescent green diving suits. I was hoping that they would stay well clear of the concrete silo but their bubble trail indicated that they were heading directly towards me. In order to avoid complications I reeled in the line until they had passed through my patch and had moved along the coastline towards Pencra Head. Porthoustock is a popular venue for the diving fraternity as the dreaded Manacles, where many a vessel has met its fate, lies just around the corner. In fact, while I'm on the subject of diving, my pal Tim Hansen gave me a large WW1 shell casing that he had salvaged from a local wreck a decade ago. The unfortunate vessel was the

British steamship 'Volnay', which had been carrying a cargo of ammunition destined for our troops fighting in the Great War in France. The 4,610-ton ship was homeward bound from Canada when there was an explosion close to her bows as she arrived off the Manacles. It was assumed that she had hit a German mine. Two tugs were sent to assist the stricken vessel but sadly she sank in the middle of the bay before any rescue attempt could take place, on 14 December 1917. Today the Volnay lies in nearly 70 feet of water on a sandy bottom. She is now well and truly broken up, with large pieces of wreckage strewn about including bollards, winches, boilers, deck plates and lots of wooden ammunition boxes!

Anyhow, the commotion caused by the divers didn't adversely affect the fishing as I had first thought and, surprisingly, bites continued just as before. The next drop down with my new fixed paternoster rig produced another Ballan of about 2¾lbs and this was followed by seven more of similar proportions. Each of these captures had to be painstakingly guided around to the beach for the landing ceremony I described previously so you may appreciate how hectic the sport was on that day – my knees were creaking by the time I had finished! In just an hour I had put together a catch of nine sizeable Ballan Wrasse and a solitary Corkwing Wrasse weighing about 4ozs. I also lost three fish in the rough ground during the non-stop activity at this prolific little Wrasse haven...

It had been one of those red-letter days that usually remain embedded in the memory box. In fact I'd also scored earlier in the day when I'd been fishing another rock mark at first light to try and secure our breakfast – there's nothing better than a couple of fresh Mackerel fillets seared in butter in a hot frying pan! Anyway, I had been struggling and couldn't get a sniff of a Mackerel using Shrimp lures so I turned to an old trick that changed my luck in an instant. Employing what the Cornish salts call a 'snaid' was a little dodge that

I'd learned from one of the all-time great skippers, the late Bernard Hunkin, who operated out of Mevagissey. Just adding a long, thin sliver of Squid to one of the hooks made all the difference in the world, producing Mackerel with every cast. Of course the best snaid to use is probably the white or silvery skin from the Mackerel itself but it wasn't necessary on this occasion. A dozen fish ensured that all the family were able to sample the delights of perhaps the most underrated of our sea fish for the following couple of days - lovely!

These powerful fish provide fabulous sport
on balanced tackle

Chapter V

Siamese Fins - January 2009

Rawson and I were chatting about the fishing in Thailand during my grandson's christening celebration, having had one beer too many, when a good idea came to mind. What was there to stop us from taking a winter break there? It was short notice but we were sure our wives wouldn't need too much encouragement! Of course our motives for travelling over 6,000 miles weren't all about visiting Buddhist temples and sunning ourselves on a tropical beach. No, it was the fantastic fishing opportunities, particularly for exotic freshwater species, that was the real attraction. A steady stream of glowing reports of captures made by my old oppo Dave Wilson, who now resides in the country, had filtered through and the temptation for us to try our luck had become too much to ignore any longer. I am pleased to say that convincing our wives of the benefits of such a trip turned out to be a mere formality and so Thailand was pencilled into the calendar – happy days!

The holiday arrangements were formulated and I wasted no time in organising a guide for a day's fishing at Sawai Lake on the island of Phuket. Everything seemed to be coming together nicely, although the timing of the venture was beginning to look somewhat questionable. Firstly, there was the 'credit crunch' and the sudden devaluation of the pound that meant our spending power was reduced by about a quarter. Secondly, the price of oil on the world markets had rocketed to 150 dollars a barrel, which impacted on the cost of the flights. And, to cap it all, there was civil unrest in the country! Political tensions were headline news across the globe and the airport in Bangkok – our first port of call – was under siege and closed to all air traffic. Whilst we could overcome the financial implications, the people's protest was a different story – the situation looked hopeless and we couldn't foresee any way through the crisis. Fortunately for us, political stability returned just in time and it was a major relief to all when we were able to continue with our holiday plans – phew, that was a close one! Our itinerary included a two-night stay in Bangkok, followed by twelve days at a little place called Karon on the south-western coast of Phuket. The accommodation at our final destination was a guest house run by my son's friend, Daniel, who also happened to be a professional deep-sea diving instructor. We were hoping that his expert knowledge of local reefs and likely fish-holding areas might prove useful to us. My intention, as ever, was to pack a telescopic rod and some bait in my backpack so I would be ready at a moment's notice to cast a line as we visited different coastal resorts. The sparkling green-blue waters of the Andaman Sea that surrounds Phuket is one of those places that I've read about on numerous occasions and have always wanted to fish – I can already sense a new species coming with every cast!

My son Lee amongst the shoals at Koh Phi Phi in the Andaman Sea - photograph courtesy of Daniel Finck

It was like entering a blast furnace as we exited the outer doors of the airport in Thailand's capital city. We had left England when temperatures were below zero and we were now basking in sunshine which was over 30°c in the shade!

Luckily, our taxi transfer was already waiting and within 45 minutes we had arrived at the Marriott Courtyard Hotel to begin our adventure. There was only one full day at our disposal which for the best part we had decided to spend on the river travelling to various places of interest. This option made sense because during the limited time-frame we would be able to see some of the major attractions as well as a cross-section of life in Bangkok.

On the day itself, as you may have expected, I packed the telescopic in case a fishing situation came my way, but this was more in hope than anything else. As things stood, the prospect of casting a line seemed remote but in truth I was desperate to catch a fish for the record from the mighty Chao Phraya River. After gorging a splendid Thai breakfast we took the Skytrain to Saphan Taksin to pick up our riverboat connection which was to ferry us to the Grand Palace and Temple of Dawn, amongst others. The sight of the river as we approached the Central Pier was just breathtaking – it was huge and had a flow to match. It powered through, carrying with it the usual flotsam of a busy city and rafts of what looked like large sections of water lilies – our immediate assumption was that these green accumulations were Water Chestnut plants but who knows! River traffic was brisk, with passenger ferries and eye-catching longtail boats going speedily about their business between the numerous 'pier stations'. The river seemed to be in a continual state of flux as wake from the vessels collided with wake and I could only imagine how big the fish could grow in such a river. Nevertheless, for the time being I had to get the idea of fishing out of my head and concentrate on our sightseeing tour of bustling Bangkok.

The riverboat voyage took us to the Maharaj Pier, where we immediately fell for the charms of a pair of tuk-tuk drivers. We had been specifically warned about the dangers of accepting lifts from chaps like these but here we were, as gullible as ever, embarking on a mystery tour! Our friendly hosts proceeded to show us around all the major sights, including the customary jewellery shops and tailors, just in case we wanted to buy a diamond ring or a suit or two! Weaving in and out of the busy traffic was great fun and, despite the embarrassment of being ushered into shops where we had no intention of making a purchase, the experience was the best thing we could have done. Regardless of our initial qualms, we not only managed to see all the main places of interest but it also gave us an insight into what everyday living in Thailand was really like – perfect!

A longtail boat cutting through the waters
of the Chao Phraya River in Bangkok

During the return journey along the river, I was scanning around for vantage points where it was possible to cast a line, but these were very few and far between. I did see a handful of anglers but most of the access to the banks seemed to be on private property or hotel frontages. I was already preparing myself for disappointment when I noticed two local lads fishing in a small gap between the embankment and the Central Pier, which happened to be our stop. This was my chance and I quickly assembled the telescopic that had been fitted up with float tackle before asking the other fellows if I could slot in on the end. They had prime position which allowed them to access the deep water downstream of the pier pilings while I had to fish in the eddying water beneath the pier itself. There was very little space but I did manage to run my float through nicely on a few occasions. The lads kept pointing out a shoal of fish that appeared periodically in the heavy current for a few seconds but I was unsure what they were. They looked like Tilapia but unfortunately I wasn't in a position to be able to cast for them – talk about frustrating! Anyway, I'd been there for about five minutes when the peacock quill shot under and I struck into a Chao Phraya Catfish, also known as the Giant Catfish. The sweetcorn that I'd brought from the UK had worked but I was a little surprised it had been a Catfish that had taken it. After looking it over for a few seconds, I released it back into the Chao Phraya, to the dismay of the Thai lads who thought it would have made a good meal! It may only have been a baby but it was my first fish caught in Thailand and it finished off the day nicely. Our brief visit to Bangkok was coming to an end and the following morning would see us heading back to the airport for a domestic flight to Phuket – things could not have got off to a better start...

We had only been in Thailand for a couple of days but the flight had given us time to reflect and there was one thing in particular that was glaringly obvious to us. This was that, in general, the Thai people had a genuinely respectful and friendly disposition. It was heart-warming to experience these traits, which I can only assume have come through their Buddhist faith which is practised by the majority of the population. The people of Phuket were no exception to this rule, although their driving habits left a lot to be desired! For example, it wasn't uncommon to see a family of four, including babies, on a small motorcycle! Whilst we're on the subject, our taxi journey from Phuket Airport to 'Baan Suay' in Karon - the guest house belonging to Daniel and his wife, Suporn – was also a bit hair-raising. High speeds and overtaking on the inside as well as the outside seemed to be normal practice, which was a little disconcerting to say the least. Albeit we did arrive safely and what a warm welcome we had waiting for us – the staff went out of their way to greet us in typical Thai tradition. It felt like home and it was good to be able to relax and settle down for a while as it seemed like we had been travelling for days. Our new environment was both comfortable and luxurious and had everything that we could possibly need to ensure our stay was a pleasurable one – get the beers in Raws! During our journey we'd only had brief glimpses of the coastline but what we had seen was spectacular – tree-covered hills and sun-drenched beaches set against a vista of azure blue. I couldn't wait to see more of it at close quarters. On a different note, however, our other observation was the alarming rate in which the places were being developed to cater for the growing tourist industry. Phuket was definitely a popular part of the country but I do hope they don't over-cook the building projects. Well, I've now set the scene so perhaps it's time for me to concentrate more on the fishing which, in the main, took place during four glorious days, starting with our special one at Sawai Lake.

Sawai Lake - 20th January

I hadn't stopped thinking about this day since it had been booked and now at last we were about to embark with our Danish freelance guide, Meik Neilsen. Our estimated time of arrival at the fishery was 8am which, as far as I was concerned, would allow us ten hours of pure, unadulterated pleasure. Meik told us a bit about the fishery and, so that we didn't get our hopes too high, also forewarned us that blank sessions do occur although these were unusual. He also gave us the latest news that meat-based baits had recently been banned by the owner of the lake, presumably because of their success rate. Apparently, the next best permissible bait, which Meik had brought along for us to use, was raw Prawns. There were many different species of fish in the lake and fortunately most of them were partial to Prawns, with bread also taking its fair share of catches. Apart from lake and jungle fishing, Meik spends much of his time on the game-fishing boats that specialise in Marlin and Sailfish. In fact, he has supervised dozens of captures that have given many of his customers trophy fish of a lifetime. It may sound a little odd to you but, whilst I'd love to have one of these grand fish credited to my name, the methods involved in catching them aren't really my cup of tea. Despite the excitement and the glamour, I much prefer the more conventional, hands-on methods of catching fish – but that's not to say that I wouldn't jump at the chance if an invitation came my way! The rush-hour traffic was heavy and so was the noise but when we turned off the main drag towards the fishing park, things soon became so tranquil you could have heard a pin drop. As we entered the site my eyes were drawn to the pool and the first thing I noticed were some big swirls occurring here and there – I had no idea what type of fish were causing them but the place looked very inviting indeed and I couldn't wait to get organised. Meik escorted us around to a hotspot where he had seen a number of good fish caught previously and, for the time being, it appeared that we had the pool to ourselves. The location was ideal and the place had been set out with anglers' comfort in mind. There was a restaurant on site and a number of Thai huts and bamboo chairs dotted around strategically for anglers to relax while they waited for the fish to bite. Unfortunately, the huts were just a little too far away from the rod rests for our liking, so we arranged our seating outside in the full glare of the unrelenting sun – you know what they say about mad dogs and Englishmen! The fishery looked just the ticket, which was more than I could say for the tackle. No complaints with the fixed spool reels loaded with 20lb breaking strain braid, but the seven foot, short-handled spinning rods could have been more appropriate in view of the calibre of the fish that we were seeking. Anyway, for the record, our end tackle consisted of a light running leger rig incorporating a size 2 hook which was attached to a heavy braided hook link. The Prawn baits were carefully positioned close to some features on the far bank about 30 yards from shore and the bale arms were opened to allow any fish taking the bait to run unheeded. To hold everything in place, a loop of line was tucked under a rubber band which had been attached to the rod butt next to the reel. As ever, I had brought along my telescopic and a tin of sweetcorn which Meik said I should put into the margins to the right of our position, giving us the chance of catching some alternative species. To round things off, Meik balled in some groundbait made with mashed bread around each of the baits and then it was a waiting game...

I was buzzing with excitement, as any capture was going to be a new freshwater personal best, but things were strangely quiet for the first hour or so. There was still quite a lot of fish movement and I was just wondering whether a surface bait might be a better bet when line started pouring off the spool of my leger rod. It was a relief when I hooked my first fish, which was bumping and boring away at the end of the line. I had no idea what it was and I could only pray that there were going to be no complications and that the hook held firm. The first glimpse I had was when the fish broke surface under the rod tip and I could have cheered with joy. It was a Pacu and the one fish I really wanted to catch. The Pirhana-like fish was just about ready for the net when it suddenly leapt clear of the water but, fortunately for me, Meik had anticipated its intentions and netted it in mid-air! Meik's fast reactions were matched by Rawson's, who managed to capture the very moment with the camera – what a team! My Pacu weighed a tad over 10lbs and I was as happy as a pig in clover.

A very special capture - a 10lb Pacu

The next action came about 20 minutes later and, luckily for me, the fish had come to my rod again. I struck and connected with something much bigger than I had anticipated which moved slowly and inexorably, without any sign of panic, as I exerted as much pressure as the line would stand. The battle soon developed into something I hadn't experienced before, which I could only liken to being attached to a juggernaut in first gear. Meik said that I had hooked an Arapaima and my only hope was that it made for the open water towards our right, but unfortunately it didn't. The monster was heading for a wooden jetty on the far bank and there was nothing I could do to change its course. Ultimately, the inevitable happened and I began to feel the line grating as the fish found the jetty's pilings before everything went slack – the fish, which probably weighed in excess of 100lbs, had made its escape.

It would seem an opportune time to give all the bird buffs amongst you a brief insight into the birdlife that we encountered on the day at Sawai lake. Apart from the Mynah Birds that were just about everywhere, we saw a few tiny birds with long curved beaks which resembled Humming Birds, three different types of Egret and a very elegant Eagle. The raptor had brown-coloured wings and a bright white head and nape, and the consensus was that it was a Fish Eagle.

Anyway, Rawson was the next one to get a run which he hit successfully. His fish gave him a right old scrap before we were able to get a glimpse of the red tailfin which confirmed its identity – a Red-Tailed Catfish. This superb-looking fish weighed 11½lbs and was netted without a problem so it was time for a little celebration as by now we had both taken double figure fish. An order went out for some Singha beer which was duly delivered by a lovely lady on a quad bike. The cool-box with several bottles of our favourite tipple immersed in a bed of ice was left with us to sample as and when we felt like it – this trip was beginning to have a heavenly feel!

*   *   *   *

Rawson displays his very handsome Red Tailed Catfish

By now, six hours had passed and I still hadn't had so much
as a nibble on the float-fished sweetcorn despite the fact
that I had been peppering the area with the particles every
quarter of an hour or so. There were plenty of fish about
and I was a little mystified as to why no fish had shown any

interest in my offering. Part of the problem could have been that the fish in the lake hadn't come across sweetcorn before because local anglers rarely use it. Meik confirmed that the bait hadn't been readily used yet although he had heard rumours of huge Siamese Carp being caught on it. Stone the crows, I hadn't bargained for such a possibility – my expectations had been for something along the lines of a Barb or Gourami! It was looking like my 5lb breaking strain monofilament could have been a bit on the light side. While sport on the float rod had been non-existent, the leger rods were seeing an increasing number of bites as the day progressed. The next fish landed was a 5½lb Striped Catfish that fell to my rod – a large chunk of bread had brought its downfall. This capture was followed by a pair of lovely Pacu weighing 8¾lbs and 10½lbs respectively, both coming to Rawson's rod, and a 3½lb Walking Catfish that fell to mine. The killing bait for the latter three fish was Prawn.

Our day was coming to an end when finally, after nine hours without a touch, the peacock quill blipped below the surface – at long last something had intercepted my sweetcorn bait. Unfortunately, by the time I reached the rod the float had returned to its normal position and it seemed that the chance had been squandered. Undeterred, I stood next to the rod and remained focused just in case I was given a second opportunity. Sure enough, within two minutes the float shot under again and, before I had time to strike, the bait runner was already conceding line as the fish hooked itself. Blimey, it was an aggressive take and I could only wonder what had taken the bait. The rod was pulled over from one side to the other as the fish dived about like a thing possessed. It was another strange fight that required my full concentration for several minutes before I was able to gain the upper hand. I had actually worked up a sweat and was relieved when Meik was able to slip the net under the lively fish that had given me the run-around in the blazing heat. The Drennan Starpoint size 8 was removed and, as with all my special captures, I took a few seconds out to admire the fish as it lay in the net. Meik said that the speed merchant was in fact a Rohu which in some respects resembled a Grass Carp, one of my favourite species. It weighed in at 6½lbs and ended one of the most enjoyable fishing sessions of my life.

Sleek and powerful with speed to match - Rohu

Coral Island and Rawai Pier – 22nd January

The girls had decided that this day would be spent at a beach location on one of the tropical islands before returning to Rawai for a seafood supper at a restaurant recommended by Daniel named 'Nong Pims 2' – oh boy, this was the life! After a fabulous Thai breakfast we grabbed a taxi to Rawai with the view of finding a boatman to take us to a quiet island for some beach relaxation. Of course, I had no intention of lazing - I would use the opportunity to try and catch some sea fish. To this end, Daniel had given me some Squid and Prawns from the freezer which were stored away safely in my backpack. Rawai was a typical coastal town with lots of bars and restaurants on one side of the road and a beautiful beach on the other. As always there were plenty of people about, ready to offer their services, and securing a longtail boat for our voyage was straightforward. A dozen or so of these wonderful vessels were moored along the shallows and, following the normal bartering routine, we soon found a skipper to take the four of us to Coral Island.

I had very much been looking forward to going on a jaunt in one of these boats, which you often see buzzing along the rivers of Asia in television documentaries. To be honest, I couldn't have contemplated going to Thailand without taking a trip in a longtail boat – it would have been like going to Venice and not seeking the services of a gondolier. Anyway, it was now about to happen and the four of us waded through the shallows before climbing aboard. The 45-minute crossing didn't disappoint and the captivating views across the calm waters of the Andaman will be something I'll never forget. Time passed quickly and before we knew it we were approaching the mooring point about a 100 yards from the shore at Coral Island. I was just thinking that we might have been expected to swim ashore when our skipper hailed a couple of lads in a rowing boat to come and ferry us to a beach that looked like something from a holiday brochure. It was a wonderful setting of white sand and coconut palms and, not only that, it appeared that apart from a few local inhabitants we had the beach to ourselves – I must say we did feel rather privileged. Believe it or not, no sooner had we settled onto the beach than our boatman sauntered over with a small offering of bread, apparently for us to feed the fish! This was now getting silly and I had to slap myself to make sure I wasn't dreaming – things couldn't get much better. We were ushered back to the shoreline and into the sea but as far as we could make out there were no visible signs of fish activity. However, my wife decided to casually throw in a slice to test the water and within seconds the place was teeming with fish competing for the bread. I was now in a state of shock – where had all these fish come from? Pointing at my rod, I enquired if I would be allowed to fish but the boatman laughingly shook his head before directing us to the next cove. I thought it was too good to be true.

Rawson and I wasted no time in collecting our stuff before setting out on a walkabout to find a place to cast a line, and it didn't take us long to do so. Clambering around the first set of rocks we came upon a promising spot that was worth a try. Using a section of Prawn on a fixed paternoster rig produced an instant result – a lovely Bream that I photographed to help with identification at a later date. This one was quickly followed by another Bream which was larger and a different species from the first one and the camera was used once again. Rawson was also catching his fair share but I was far too busy to monitor the details of his captures. With each cast we found that we were edging out further into the sea, trying to keep in closer touch with the fish, and before we knew it we were waist deep. Fishing in this manner was a new experience and one that I wouldn't be repeating around our own coastline. Anyway, the sport was fast and furious, with bites occurring as soon as the bait hit bottom, and my next capture was a Wrasse. This beauty was followed by a yellow and black striped fish that I decided to take around the headland to show the girls. Taking care not to keep it out of the water for too long, I gradually paddled my way back to the spot for the demonstration but the response was slightly discouraging. The women must have taken all of two seconds to scrutinise the pretty fish before getting back to the land of Nod – so much for my efforts! Undeterred, I returned to Rawson where we continued to exploit our opportunity, although by now the captures were producing species that we had already encountered. After a further half-hour of non-stop action we were both in need of some liquid refreshment so we called time and joined our other halves on the beach. It had been an enjoyable and productive session and the good news was that we still had some bait left!

'Bream on' - there's nothing like getting
up-close and personal!

At 4pm the longtail boatman came over to tell us that it was time to return to Rawai. Our little break on the island had seemed to whizz by and we were now ready for our meal, but our table at Nong Pims 2 had been booked for 6.30pm. Oh dear, this left us with an hour to kill at Rawai – ha ha! It didn't take me too long to convince the girls that an hour's fishing might be the best way to spend the spare time. It appeared they were happy to be entertained for a while so, as soon as we made our return, we went directly to the pier. The concrete construction was an ideal venue because it was only five minutes walk away from the restaurant and also there seemed to be plenty going on to keep the women happy. I was a little disappointed however to discover that the only deep water to be had was at the very end of the pier, where it seemed that everyone and his dog had gathered. There were rodsmen, netsmen and fishermen with hand lines crammed into every nook and cranny, leaving no room for us to cast our lines. Frustratingly, my eyes were glued to the catches that had been laid out for all to see, including a whole array of different species and one very handsome Trigger Fish – how I would have loved to have caught that one! Some quick thinking was required if I was to increase my own species tally. The sea leading up to the end of the pier had been shallow and somewhat barren but I did remember passing one small feature about half way down. It was just an old piece of rope covered in seaweed but the twisted coils had created a few pockets of refuge that I felt certain would hold some fish – this had to be my only chance. I soon found the little haven again and opted for float tackle and a sliver of Squid to try and draw out a fish or two. Within two minutes the quill was sliding away and I latched onto a stunning Sea Perch which once again required some digital photography to assist with identification. The next fish up was a Bream which was identical to one I had caught earlier on Coral Island, and the final fish of the day was a second Sea Perch. Grasping this little window of opportunity had once again paid dividends – it was now time for our seafood extravaganza!

Saw-Jaw Monocle Bream

Sergeant Major Fish

Beach at Karon – 27th January

This was another opportunistic situation which came about when Daniel invited us to join his family on the beach for a picnic at sunset. In this part of the world the sun sinks below the horizon very quickly and the experience was apparently awesome. The arrangement was for Daniel to ferry us all down to the beach in his 4x4 after he had collected the children from school, and this went like clockwork. We arrived at a spot midway along the huge expanse of sand where we were able to set up our temporary residence with the rest of the sun worshippers. All the usual beach paraphernalia was brought along, including a couple of large well-stocked cool boxes for good measure. Even though it was evening time the temperature was still surprisingly high and there was no need to wear anything more than swim shorts. I was beginning to get a little envious of Danny as this was just part and parcel of everyday routine for him – he certainly had the life of Riley! Our picnic had been prepared by Suporn in advance and what a treat we had in store. A tropical fruit buffet consisting of bite-sized pieces of mango, rambutan, durian, mangosteen, dragon fruit, water melon, roseapples, pineapple, coconut and miniature bananas was laid out invitingly for us to sample – mangosteen was without doubt my favourite!

The frivolities continued as the beer flowed and before we knew it the sun was going down, creating a wonderful reddish haze across the horizon. We gathered along the shoreline to take in the aura of the event and, after the customary photographs, it was time at last to get the rods out. In view of the fact that our intention had been to fish at dusk, Rawson had already made up his mind to try his luck for a Squid using a brightly-coloured lure that he had purchased locally. The lure, which incorporated a built-in weight, was about five inches in length and was meant to represent the Squid's main prey of Shrimps and Prawns. We were surprised to find that it didn't actually contain a treble hook as such but had a collar of wire grippers in which the Squid's tentacles were supposed to become entangled – I must say that I had my doubts. This was Rawson's first attempt at these strange sea creatures but I wasn't going to follow suit this time.

I had decided to stick with orthodox leger tackle to try and winkle out some more new species. In any event, it seemed like a good opportunity for us to don our new straw hats which we had bought from a street hawker in the famous 'Bangla Road' during a visit to the lively town of Patong - lively being the operative word! The hats caused quite a stir in Patong with just about everyone making funny comments and generally ridiculing us as we sauntered through the streets. Now as we walked down towards the shore we probably looked like a pair of Vietnamese coolies ready to start work in the paddy fields - but what the hell!

'Fishing in the twilight'

As we began fishing, it was reassuring to see a couple of local fishermen approaching who also had Squid in mind. The fact that they were about to use lures similar to the one Rawson had selected confirmed that these marine predators could be caught off Karon beach. Up to that point we had been unsure whether Cephalopods would actually be present in a shallow, sandy environment. While Rawson's confidence had risen a few notches with the good tidings, I was struggling to get a bite on my Squid offering, which was unlike the instantaneous action I had experienced on Coral Island. In fact, it was a good ten minutes before the rod was tapping and my first fish was beached. It looked like a Snapper or a Sea Perch but I was pleased to see that it differed from the ones taken at Rawai – great stuff, it was another new mark. As I sit in my snow-bound home writing this piece, with the vivid memories of the pair of us standing fishing in the warm Andaman Sea, I have a compelling desire to be back in Thailand again – the place has certainly got me hooked! Anyway, reverting back, Rawson was taking a leaf out of the Thai boys' book by slowing down his retrieve and introducing some jigging movement into the process which took a bit of getting used to. The lure kept touching bottom which in turn upset the rhythm, making life difficult for him, but he persevered and gradually found a way to present the lure suitably in the shallow water. In the meantime, I had caught a second Sea Perch but bites were still few and far between so I tried a shorter cast to see if that would bear fruit and it did – a gentle bite produced a fish that resembled a cross between a Dragonet and a small Bonefish. I was delighted with this capture as it was a welcome change from the usual Bream and Perch. Anyhow, as I was about to release it, there was a sudden whoop of excitement as Rawson latched onto something that had taken the lure about 40 yards from shore. He began recovering line as fast as he dared and we waited eagerly to see what was going to appear at the end of the line. I love the suspense of a situation like this, especially when it ends triumphantly as it did here. Rawson's determination had paid off and his glee was clearly perceptible, which isn't a common occurrence. His day was really made when Suporn offered to take his precious catch back to the kitchen staff at Baan Suay with a view to having it prepared for his breakfast – Thai noodle soup with a side dish of freshly-fried Squid – lovely!

Confucius he say -
'Everything has its beauty but not everyone sees it'

Beach at Kata – 29th January

It was getting near the end of the holiday and I was hungry for a last opportunity to cast a line somewhere. I'd already had my fair share of fishing and so I wasn't looking forward to requesting yet another bout, especially as last minute shopping was likely to be on the agenda. However, remembering the old adage 'If you don't ask, you don't get,' I finally plucked up enough courage to pose the question over breakfast. Fortunately our good ladies were surprisingly sympathetic to my plea. As long as the destination was going to be somewhere we hadn't already visited, we would be allowed an hour or so to do our thing. The question now was where to go. I managed to catch Daniel before he left on the school run and he suggested that we went to Kata. Apparently he had dived on the reef that extends from a point on the shoreline to way out into the Andaman. There was some very deep water, particularly on the sea-ward side of the reef, but the problem was that we were going to need mountaineering boots to get there! We were warned that, in order to reach the mark at the spot where the reef touches the shore, we would have to carry out some tricky manoeuvring across some formidable rock formations. Despite this minor setback, the proposal sounded ideal as we hadn't been to Kata before and furthermore it wasn't too far away. We concluded that the challenge was too good to miss and so Daniel hurriedly sketched a map for us before we set out to find a tuk-tuk driver.

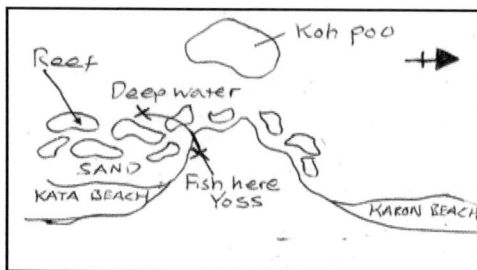

We were dropped off in Kata adjacent to a 'Tsunami Evacuation' sign, which was a sobering reminder of the terrible event that devastated many coastal communities in 2004.   Whilst the rebuilding programme had all but been completed, the memories of the thousands of people affected have been irreparably scarred. Stories of personal tragedy were never far away and it was likely to remain that way for the next generation. Looking out across the bay, I could see exactly where we needed to make for and, not only that, I was also able to determine the rough position of the reef. Small boats and diving buoys were dotted along a line which started close to the shore and stretched across the front of the beach for several hundred yards. Having established our bearings, we set out on our trudge towards the rocks to the right of the beach. As luck would have it, when we had almost reached our destination our paths crossed with a Thai chap who was struggling to carry both his surf board and his fishing equipment to the sea. He was a little surprised when I off-loaded my own stuff to help him with this task but all the while I couldn't help wondering how he was going to attempt to fish from a surf board. When we reached the sea it soon became evident that he was going to trawl a lure along the outer edge of the reef using his own paddling power!   His board had been customised so that his rod could be propped up vertically like those on any sport boat – now that's ingenuity for you. I wished him good luck and bade him farewell before returning to the girls who had settled on a couple of sunbeds. It was time for some mountaineering!

Scrambling across the boulders was relatively easy at first but it got progressively more difficult the further we went. The distance to the fishing point was about 300 yards and after about 20 minutes of arduous slog we had only covered a third of the way. It wouldn't have been quite so bad had our hands been free, but carrying the fishing gear had put paid to that. As the going got more precipitous I found that I needed to weigh up the possibility of fishing a great mark against ending up in hospital or worse. Rawson could have continued further but, having had knee replacement surgery a few months previously, I was unable to carry on. Failing to make the deep water was like a form of torture to me but at least there was a juicy-looking bay sitting directly in front of us. It wasn't particularly deep water but there were plenty of sandy channels between some lofty rocks which I felt would hold some nice fish.

Enterprising stuff - a man sets out to troll a lure along
the reef at Kata on a surfboard!

Rawson set up a spider float rig which he wanged out with a Prawn and Squid cocktail bait while I used a light leger with a three-inch strip of Squid. Almost immediately I had a fast double tap and hooked a lovely Bream which looked similar to one of the fish I had caught on Coral Island – it was lucky that I'd packed the camera. The skies were clear and it was very hot: in fact we'd heard that the temperature had actually reached 42°C. I don't think that either of us had ever experienced heat as ferocious as that before and I was gasping for a drink. Anyway, we lost sight of Rawson's float so he immediately tightened down and struck into a good fish but unfortunately it got into the rocks and he was forced to pull for a break. In the meantime, the fish were biting like mad in the 'alley' where I was placing my bait and my next fish was a nice Wrasse that took a Prawn. It was fantastic fishing but I did notice that the tide was dropping fast and I wondered how long the fish would remain there. My next cast produced one heck of a pull on a Squid bait but the hook link snapped on the strike and I had to spend valuable time re-tackling. Time was running out as the tide receded but we did manage to catch a number of Bream before the bite rate dropped off dramatically. The last few casts were made in a new spot to my right where I caught a beautifully-marked Rockfish that had some vicious spines, and a pair of striped fish shaped like Chub. If I'd had more time at my disposal I would have run a small rubber Eel through some of the juicy-looking channels between the rocks but perhaps that will have to wait until next time. It had been a fabulous session and now it was time for a well-earned drink.

Monogrammed Monocle Bream

White Spotted Rabbit Fish/ Spinefoot

The holiday was over as far as fishing was concerned but I still had the task of identifying the sea-fish that I had caught in order to update my fishing logbook. My first route is normally to consult the reference books that I've collected over the years which cover different species of fish from various places around the world. In the main these are 'divers' books containing detailed photographs together with some background facts and, more importantly, the Latin names. Another useful avenue is the Internet which provides a wealth of information, although some of the pictures or names put on by amateur enthusiasts are not always accurate. A better option is probably to refer to some of the dedicated 'fish-based' websites that are invariably very comprehensive. Anyway, Daniel was able to help me with a couple of my captures but the majority were named by an old colleague, Andy Pearson, who is madder than me when it comes to fishing. He is definitely a man after my own heart as he travels here, there and everywhere in pursuit of the watery beasts. However he is much more successful at it than me and I would suggest that anyone who is interested in Andy's exploits should visit his very professional website (**www.gulliblestravels.co.uk**) – you won't be disappointed!

For the record, the identification of the sea-fish that I caught in Thailand are, at the time of writing, listed below with their place of capture:

Lagoon Damsel Fish .... **Nai Harm**
(*Hemiglyphidodon plagiometopon*)
Monogrammed Monocle Bream ..... **Coral Island/Kata**
(*Scolopsis monogramma*)
Sergeant Major Fish .... **Coral Island**
(*Abudefduf saxatilis*)
Saw-Jawed Monocle Bream . **Coral Island/Rawai Pier**
(*Scolopsis ciliata*)

Russells Snapper/Moses Perch .... **Rawai Pier**
(Lutianus russelli)
Crescent Banded Grunter .... **Karon**
(Terapon jarbua)
Asian Sillago .... **Karon/Phi Phi Island**
(Sillago asiatica)
Cooks Cardinal Fish .... **Kata**
(Apogon cookii)
White Spotted Rabbit Fish/Spinefoot .... **Kata**
(Siganus canaliculatus)
Diamond Wrasse .... **Kata**
(Haliochoeres dossumieri)

One other Wrasse was caught on Coral Island that I have been unable to identify as yet.

The Kingdom of Thailand was certainly a fun place to visit and I would love to go back again sometime with a view to exploring a different area. For some reason, since returning to England, I have been unable to shake the sight of the awesome rivers out of my head. I expect the reason is that, for all intents and purposes, these waterways are 'untapped' and the potential for catching a whole new range of freshwater species could almost be a formality. In particular, I would like to target the different types of Barb and Carp as well as Tilapia, Featherbacks, Snakeheads, Gourami, Thai Mahseer and even the mighty Mekong Catfish! Yes, just the thought of it makes the hair on the back of my neck tingle. Long may Thailand remain just the way it is today – the memories of the lovely people, their culture, the bustling night bazaars, the climate, the tropical island paradises and, above all (apart from the fishing that is), the wonderful seafood cuisine, will remain with me always.

Chapter VI

The Annual Dartmouth Plaice Festival – 18th and 19th April 2009

Since witnessing the high number and the quality of the elegant flatfish caught in the 2008 competition, I have been champing at the bit for an opportunity to have a go myself. However, my fellow compatriots had warned me not to build my hopes up too much because history has shown that this particular event has notoriously been affected by the weather. Most of the fishing takes place on the Skerries Bank which is totally dependent on the prevailing winds and tide. The dreaded scenario is when the weather people predict winds from an easterly direction, and this is for two reasons: firstly, it kills sport stone dead and, secondly, there is no protection whatsoever on the banks and fishing can become practically impossible in these circumstances. In fact, the whole procedure is in the 'lap of the gods' until virtually the day before the festival is actually due to take place. Despite the uncertainties, the contest is still very popular, attracting anglers from far afield to vie for a specimen fish and the lucrative awards. Anyway, before getting down to the nitty gritty, the time might be opportune for me to provide some background information regarding the general fishing area.

The Skerries Bank lies in Start Bay in more or less a straight line from Start Point to within a few miles of Dartmouth. Depths on the main bank range from 40 to 90 feet which, apart from the Plaice, is an ideal habitat for Ray, Brill and Turbot. The bank itself incorporates an undulating labyrinth of gulleys and depressions that provides a natural nursery environment for a whole variety of sea creatures including juvenile Sand Eels - the fish most predators love to feed on.

Having spawned in deeper water, the Plaice return to the bank to feed on the rich pickings in early April in order to recondition themselves before disappearing again at the end of June. (Incidentally, some say that the Plaice are not worth catching until they have 'tasted May water' because they can be a bit on the thin side after spawning.) There is some speculation as to where they go: some say that they follow the Sand Eels but, either way, they return again in July and remain on the bank until the end of October. In light of these activities, it is not surprising that Spring and Autumn are the favourite times to fish for the Plaice, with the larger specimens seemingly showing in the Autumn. The general consensus is that relatively small tides of around four metres are best, as anything much bigger can create problems when presenting the bait in the tide rush across the shallow water. As I have said earlier, easterly winds are shunned by many of the anglers because catch rates are so poor. I believe that the Skerries Bank was formed by tons of sand and shingle that had been deposited as a result of the powerful tidal vortex that exists there. It can be a dangerous area to navigate and hundreds of vessels have come to grief over the centuries in the perilous waters. Whilst on the subject of tragedy, there are also a couple of historical disasters that have occurred in this locality.

Firstly, in 1896, dredging of the Skerries Bank began in order to build a new dockyard at Plymouth. With 650,000 tons of shingle removed, wave energy gradually increased, washing away the shingle beach at a little place called Hallsands, which had the effect of leaving the village exposed to storms. On 26th January 1917 the entire village, with the exception of one house, was destroyed in a heavy storm and the area has virtually remained deserted until the present time. The ruins of many of the buildings can still be viewed from a small observation platform set into the cliffs.

Secondly, the long shingle beach at Slapton was the chosen site for 'Operation Tiger' prior to the D-Day landings in

WWII. More than 900 American service personnel lost their lives during an amphibious landing exercise when German E -boats attacked the allied ships. The whole episode was kept a closely-guarded secret for fear of undermining morale at such a critical time in the war and could have led to a postponement of the invasion.

*   *   *   *

Time was going on but despite my efforts I had still been unable to make any firm arrangements to fish in the 2009 festival. Rawson wanted to join me on the weekend jaunt but we were having difficulty finding a couple of spare slots on a charter boat. The problem was that they had already been reserved by the anglers who fish in the contest year-on-year. Our plans had been thwarted but we were still determined to give it our best shot even if it meant travelling down and taking pot luck. I was a little reluctant to do so but, as a last resort, I got in touch with my old friend Johnny Chick who runs a tackle shop in Dartmouth. I knew that Johnny was going to be very busy ensuring that all the competitors had adequate bait and tackle so I wasn't expecting any breakthrough, but at least there was a glimmer of hope. In view of his commitments he was obviously unable to fish on the Saturday but he had made up his mind to fish for a few hours on the Sunday, weather permitting. The good news was that both Rawson and myself were invited along to join him but the bad news was that the weather wasn't looking too good. Saturday's forecast was for light north-easterly winds and drizzle, which was far from ideal. Sunday was more of the same except that the skies were clearing and we could expect a sun tan. Despite the doubts about getting out, Rawson and I decided to make the journey to Dartmouth the night before and, on arrival, registered for the contest along with the rest of the lads...

Dartmouth Annual Plaice Festival 2009

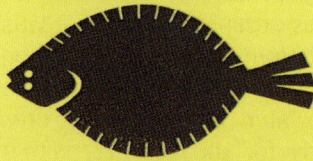

DARTMOUTH ANGLING & BOATING ASSOCIATION

Saturday 18th & Sunday 19th April 2009

Even though we weren't going to be actively involved in the fishing on day one of the festival, I was keen to get a feel for things so we thought an early morning stroll to the tackle shop was a good starting point.   As expected,

Johnny was busily packaging up Ragworms and Squid in readiness for the punters who were about to invade his establishment. Already I could sense that there was a buzz of excitement developing and it wouldn't be long before the rest of the townsfolk would be caught up in the general hubbub of the occasion. As Johnny's customers began to drift in, my feeling was that most of them were probably oblivious as to who they were actually dealing with – until now that is. Not many people are privy to the fact that Johnny's somewhat illustrious title is Lord John Arthur Charles Bingham-Chick – now there's a name for you! Blimey - who would have thought that I'd end up fishing in 'higher circles' one day! Anyway, Johnny was still concerned about the weather and concluded that his dory might be a little on the light side if conditions deteriorated any further. However, it was accepted that there was nowt we could do about it, apart from keeping one eye on the weather glass and our fingers firmly crossed. Time was quickly rolling on and an hour later the anglers were gathering on the quayside, ready for the off. As with all contests of this nature, the highly-charged atmosphere of excitement and optimism was clearly perceptible. I thought that it might be a good idea to have a chat with some of the lads to glean some tips, so I decided to muscle my way into a mêlée of anglers. During this brief window of opportunity I heard all sorts of tales, mainly about bait, which varied considerably from Ragworms and Shellfish to Mussels and long fillets of Launce. However, the best piece of information seemed to be that the biggest mistake made by anglers fishing on the Skerries was not using enough lead. Apparently the tidal thrust across the shallow banks is severe and the sinker can be propelled off the bottom as it increases in strength, destroying any chance of fish finding the bait. It was imperative to keep the weight on the sea-bed at all times, which means alternating the size of the lead in accordance with the power of the tide. This was sound advice and I would certainly be bearing it in mind. By now the pontoon was chock full of fishing boats ready to embark for the fishing grounds, including a few that I'd read about over the years in the angling press. One in particular that had stuck in my mind was 'Salt Wind', skippered by the veteran Lloyd Saunders – now there's a seaman with a grand reputation!

Sea Angler II - first in line and ready to head out of the River Dart bound for the Skerries

After breakfast Rawson and I took a drive around the coast to Torcross where we hoped to keep tabs on the flotilla of fishing boats out at sea. It was overcast and the horizon was hazy but we could just make out the large group of vessels that were fishing at the Start Point end of the bank. The north-easterly may have only been light but it was bitterly cold standing on the exposed beach. 'White horses' were beginning to show on the crest of the waves and in some respects we were relieved not to have been fishing out there with them. Not only that, we were also glad when we got back to the warm comfort of the car – what a pair of butterflies! Next stop was the 'Open Arms' pub at Chillington for a couple of pints of local ale to raise our spirits and allow us the chance to talk up our prospects of going out the following morning.

The first of the boats returned to port just before 5pm and the rest were soon following on up the River Dart in readiness for the weigh-in which was to be carried out at the foot of the steps leading into the Dartmouth Angling Clubhouse. The fishing can be fabulous during these April festivals when conditions are favourable but it was soon evident that the north-easterly had taken its toll this time. The general catch rates and size of the Plaice were very much reduced compared to previous years' results but that's how the cookie crumbles sometimes. It can be difficult to accept the disappointing experiences but, let's face it, if fishing was predictable all the time it would lose much of its appeal. The problem for me though was that I seemed to be getting the rough end of the stick much too often these days. Anyway, each competitor was allowed to weigh in their best two fish of the day, providing that the length exceeded 11 inches. This strict minimum size limit is helping to safeguard future stocks and anyone attempting to present an undersized Plaice would be subject to disqualification. I have noticed that an increasing number of anglers are now returning their catches to the sea after the weighing ceremony and I must say that this is a commendable practice in my book. In fact, at the end of the 2008 contest, I witnessed one angler who went to great lengths to return a specimen Plaice that must have weighed well over 4lbs – I was heartened by such action. Unfortunately, this year's stalwarts had a leaner time of things but those who were lucky enough to catch began making their way to the clubhouse for the weigh-in. Most of the fish seemed to be between 1½ and 2½ lbs which wasn't bad considering conditions, although no specimen fish were brought to the scales. Just seeing these beautiful Flatfish at close quarters was like being beckoned by the Sirens to me and I was praying that we would be able to have a crack at them the following morning.

One of several 2lb plus Plaice weighed-in

At precisely 8am Lord Chick rang to say that he was willing to sail but once again it was looking like there was going to be an unfavourable easterly element in the winds – drat and double drat! The wind direction was frustrating but at least the sun would be shining. On a more positive note, the organisers had specifically chosen dates when there were going to be neap tides, which was certainly going to help our cause and could save the day. As we loaded all the kit onto Johnny's dory, I was reminded of my previous visit to Dartmouth in September. On that occasion we had gone out fishing for a couple of hours on the 'east grounds' and, oh boy, did we catch some Bass on Shad lures – the action had been non-stop all the way. It had been great fun vying for position with all the other fishing boats on a piece of water about the size of a football pitch. The friendly banter, leg-pulling and rivalry between the anglers was pure entertainment and I somehow felt privileged to have been there amongst Johnny's friends and fishing associates – it was like a family gathering at sea! Anyway, reverting back, about half an hour before the fishing could commence at 9am, a succession of fishing boats began to cast off and head towards the bay – day two of the competition was under way.

There had been a slight change in the wind direction but unfortunately it was now coming straight from the east, which couldn't have been worse. Things were going to be tough and under the circumstances Johnny felt that our best approach was to begin at the 'Bell Buoy' end of the banks. Apparently some of the anglers fishing the previous day had caught a number of Plaice near some Crab pots on the edge of the bank where the water was deeper. Our boat may have been smaller than the other fishing boats but she certainly wasn't any slower. As soon as we had passed Dartmouth Castle, the throttle was opened and the hull of 'Billy Bones' crashed through the waves like a speedboat. I suppose that it took us about 15 minutes to reach the Skerries 'Bell Buoy' which has been positioned at the outer edge of the bank to provide an audible warning to the boating fraternity of the shallow water hazard. We soon located the Crab pots and Johnny positioned the boat so as to avoid the ropes attached to the pots in readiness, along with several other boats, for the first drift of the day. Our bait consisted of a selection of Ragworms, Squid, Peeler Crab, King Prawns and, believe it or not, a large jar of garlic mayonnaise. Apparently, Johnny and his cohorts have been taking large numbers of Plaice, including some clonkers over the years, on Prawns that have been daubed with the stuff. I was left in no doubt about the effectiveness of this unusual combination that they really swear by! The three of us were using two hook rigs in conjunction with the usual long flowing traces and attractor beads, with a 15lb breaking strain main line. As an assortment of baits was lowered over the side to the sea floor, I forgot all about the dreaded easterly breeze that was making life so uncomfortable for us. My initial ploy was to use the lightest lead possible to hold bottom and so I began with 2ozs, but this choice soon proved inadequate. It certainly hit bottom when the reel was put into free spool but, as the boat moved on the wind, the lead was swept up into mid-water despite the extra line being surrendered. In fact it wasn't long before we were using 12ozs and still we weren't convinced that our baits were on the bottom. At first the rod would be tapping as the lead tripped across the shingle but within a minute this sensation would peter out and more line would be released to try and find bottom again. It was a difficult situation and the boat was moving so fast that we couldn't imagine the Plaice being able to take a bait even if they were feeding. Rawson was lucky to take a Whiting in the deep water section and my hooks were cleaned but that was the closest we came on the first drift, which must have taken us a couple of miles in a relatively short space of time. My mind kept wandering back to the advice I had been given - to get the bait on the bottom at all costs – but I still wasn't confident that this was the case. More and yet more lead was utilised during the next few drifts but we were moving so rapidly that we couldn't be sure that we were fishing properly – in any case, we weren't getting any bites. As Johnny was taking us back towards the 'Bell Buoy' for a fourth time, he pulled alongside some of the other boats to ascertain how his fishing buddies were faring. The response was the same every time – no bites and no Plaice. It was sombre news although in some respects it was reassuring to learn that it wasn't only us who weren't catching. Even Lordy, Sid and Squeaky, who know every inch of the banks and never return empty-handed, were fishless and despondent. Incidentally, just in case you were wondering, Squeaky got his nickname because his reel squeaks! I don't think Matt Dawson of rugby fame, who was also fishing on the bank at the time, had done any better either. Nevertheless, we fished on because the latest weather flash indicated that the wind could drop away later in the day, which could change our fortunes. However, after about five hours without so much as a bite we felt that we had been battered enough and decided to call it a day. It was disappointing but we had given it everything and there was nothing further we could have done to improve our chances.

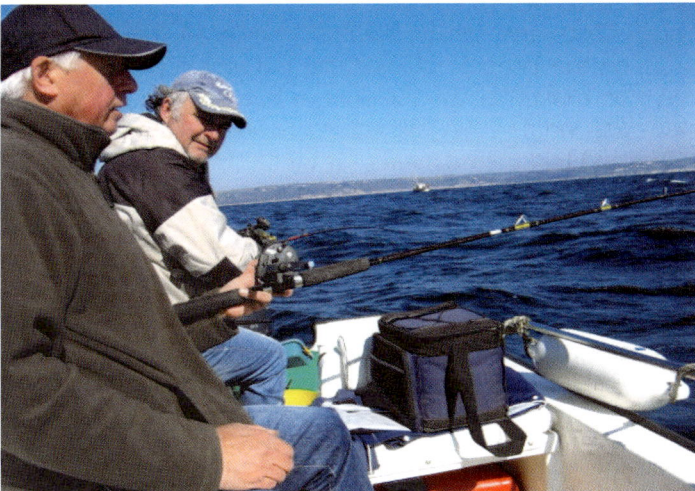

*   *   *   *   *   *

The hardest thing to swallow came later that evening, after we had returned home. Johnny contacted us to say that the wind did in fact subside just after our return to Dartmouth and, for the last hour of the contest, the Plaice had come on the feed with a vengeance. Many of the anglers were able to capitalise, including Lordy who boated ten Plaice and an enormous Brown Crab for his efforts – would you believe it! This sequence of events is so typical of my luck and it just goes to show that no matter how much planning and preparation one does it cannot always guarantee success. The winning fish for the two-day festival went under 3lbs, which is small in comparison with previous results – all right, stop crying, there's always next year!

Chapter VII

Crucian Capers - June 2009

My pal Rawson's passion is sea fishing so I was a bit taken aback when he approached me to see if I could put him on to some decent Crucian Carp. He'd caught small ones as a kid and for some reason he now had a sudden urge to try for some larger ones. I think it was all to do with that old village pond thing – you remember, the black silt and wellie boots, the duck weed and delicate bites on porcupine quills. I can fully understand this desire as our early memories of these handsome fish always leave us with a lasting impression. Anyway, it was the least I could do for my old buddy, who has accompanied me on missions all over the place on umpteen occasions. Yes, I would look forward to our assignment but the first question was where to go. We discussed a few local possibilities before selecting a nice little water tucked away in a corner of the Gloucestershire countryside. It was a typical Crucian lake with plenty of water lilies and natural features which can normally be relied upon to turn up a nice Crucian or two up to about 2lbs.

On the day we arrived at our chosen venue, there was a light southerly wind blowing, atmospheric pressure was high and everything looked rosy for a good day's fishing. We actually had the place to ourselves and we soon settled in to a couple of pitches on either side of a bed of water lilies. Some light particle feed was introduced before following it with our insert wagglers about a rod length out in five feet of water. Bait was three small Brandling worms presented on a size 14 which I've found to be the best combination to catch these shy biting fish at this venue.   Nevertheless, things turned out to be abnormally quiet – after two hours there hadn't been any tell-tale bubbling or any fish movement whatsoever and we began to think that something was amiss. The lack of activity was unusual to say the least and I wondered if the fish were spawning, although there was no visible indication of this. We continued to fish hard until the mid-afternoon without result when, all of a sudden, for no apparent reason, I found myself fully alert and expecting action at any moment. My sense 'number six', which has served me well over the years, had kicked in and somehow I just knew that a fish had entered into the target zone, despite there being no evidence of this. I wasn't surprised therefore when, within a minute, the float bobbed and then slipped beneath the surface. I struck and played what I thought was a huge Crucian Carp which I managed to net without problem on the fine tackle. On closer inspection, the fish didn't look quite right. There were gold markings on its underside and I came to the conclusion that I'd caught a hybrid rather than a true Crucian. What a shame, as the fish would have been a personal best.

My Brown Goldfish that weighed 3lb 7ozs

There have been many occasions when I've experienced 'intuitive' sensations like this latest occurrence, but each time I'm left a little numb because I haven't been able to apply any logic to it. I understand however that everybody possesses the indefinable 'sixth sense' but very few use or have knowingly experienced it. The subject is fascinating, if not a bit scary, and I have thought about it a lot as I've got older. Whilst we are on this point, I would like to tell you about another incident that happened to my daughter Siân when she was driving home through country lanes one late evening. Again for no apparent reason, she suddenly had the foresight that a Badger was about to run out in front of her car. The feeling was so strong that she actually reduced the speed of her vehicle significantly and, within seconds of rounding the next bend in the road, old Brock appeared in the headlight beams.   The fact that she actually took evasive action would indicate to me that her experience must have been compelling. It was her very first sighting of a wild Badger and the event was certainly more than just coincidence – spooky, eh?

Anyway, in view of the fact that we had only caught one hybrid between us on the first attempt to get Rawson a chunky Crucian, it now meant that I needed to come up with an alternative venue fast. Of course I knew a couple of other local fisheries where there were some reasonably-sized Crucians but I couldn't afford the time to leave it to chance again. In fact, when thinking about it, there was really no contest - it had to be Marsh Farm in Surrey, probably Britain's number one Crucian fishery. There were some real clonkers to be had there and it was just the place for Rawson to satisfy his impulsive ambitions. It would mean a fair bit of travelling in one day but, taking everything into account, it was going to be worth every drop of petrol and time.

The traffic between Bracknell and Godalming was horrendous and we didn't arrive at the fishery gates until nearly 9am – an hour and a half behind schedule. I was hoping that my favourite pegs on Harris Pool were still vacant and fortunately we found that they were. Normally I'm a stickler for adhering to proven methods but, on this occasion, I was opting for a slight change. Instead of a pellet approach I was going for an all-out caster assault - I'd heard that this versatile bait had been sorting out the better fish and I wanted to try it out for myself. Rawson decided to stick with hookable pellets that he had brought along, in a range of flavours from strawberry to bloodworm. We were both using soft-actioned match rods to cushion the impact of a good fish on our light lines and these were fitted up with pole floats attached bottom end only to combat drag. For some reason Harris Lake always seems to catch every whisper of wind which can seriously affect the presentation of light float tackle. On the face of things it looked like our float choice was going to be just about manageable in the current conditions. This was a bit of a relief because I'm not fond of anything heavier for Crucians and I'm not in favour of using a lead at this venue. It was soon clearly evident that the varied bird life at Marsh Farm was still thriving – apart from the large numbers of water fowl, there seemed to be a continual aerial conflict going on between either Little Terns, who were mobbing Herons and Magpies, and Jackdaws doing the same to Kestrel and Buzzards – you couldn't get bored at this place!

Talk about fast work – no sooner had Rawson positioned the float on his very first cast than he was trying to subdue a rod bender that just would not come to the surface. I looked on in bewilderment, thinking of the hours we had spent biteless at the Gloucestershire venue – surely it couldn't be his prize fish already? This was Rawson's story alright as the fish turned out to be a Crucian Carp weighing 3lbs on the button. Wow, he had achieved his goal in a big way with a fish that I would deem to be a specimen – what a start! At first we thought it was a Tench but when it kept plodding along the bottom under the rod tip we were more optimistic that it just might be his target fish. After a couple of photographs it was straight back to the fishing and, make no bones about it, I was already having big problems. Feeding casters must have brought the lake's entire Rudd population onto my patch – it was thick with them. Every time I introduced some loosefeed the water boiled and I was unable to get my bait to the bottom without catching Rudd. Even putting three or four on the hook didn't deter these voracious fish - they just wouldn't move on. After catching probably 50 of the things I stopped fishing for a while to rest the swim and couldn't stop wondering how other anglers catch Crucians with casters in this pool – it certainly wasn't possible to fish them all out. In the meantime, Rawson was getting a few tentative bites which he had been unable to hit, with strawberry pellets seemingly bringing most of them. By now he had already done his bit and was taking a more relaxed role while I was still working hard to pave the way for some Crucians. Discarding the casters after the pause, I turned to feeding miniature fishmeal pellets but the Rudd were still waiting and I was unable to penetrate the shoals – blimey, it was like breaking through a frenzied Piranha attack! It was time for a move.

There was a small bed of lily pads a couple of pegs further on from where Rawson was fishing that I thought looked promising, so I plonked myself down there. First job was to place some feed on the shelf in about two feet of water, about a rod length out, and fortunately there were no visible signs of Rudd activity. At last it appeared that I had got some particles in place to attract the bottom feeders – so far, so good. My hook was baited with half a Dendrobaena worm and I cast to a spot behind a clump of Yellow Flags. This was much more like it and my confidence rose several notches as I awaited developments. It seemed that my decision to move had been a sound one, although the bites that began were very cagey affairs and few were strikable. However, after half an hour or so, I did manage to connect with a two-pounder that was landed safely – a welcome Crucian but certainly not a big fish by Harris Pool standards. The catch had given my spirits a lift but, as the afternoon progressed, bites became even fewer and farther between than before. Nevertheless, it transpired that we weren't the only ones to be suffering with this lack of action. Chatting to the other anglers, it appeared that everyone was struggling for bites on the day – the Crucians were just not having it, as they say. However, it has to be appreciated that the pool receives a lot of attention from anglers and one can't expect hectic sport every time. Anyway, as far as I was concerned, the main objective had been realised: Rawson had caught his 'big 'un' and he was as happy as a Lark!

The temperature dropped considerably as evening approached and it had been a long day so we decided to give it a further half hour before tacklin' down and heading for home. I still had the best part of a pint of casters left and was tempted to introduce some again but thought better of it – I'd already had a bellyful of Rudd and didn't want to take the risk during the final spell. However, despite the fact that I would be continuing with the pellet, there was no doubt in my mind that the Crucians had 'wised up' to this bait in its many forms. The finicky attention that we had been experiencing, even on our ultra-light rigs, meant that they had become wary of it. Anyway, nothing of consequence happened during the first 20 minutes and then my float buried confidently for the first time and I hooked into a solid force that was unstoppable on my outfit. I assumed that it was one of the big Tench that can often turn up in this water. It crossed through the next swim on its initial run, some ten yards away, and then threw the hook – life can be cruel sometimes! That was it for me but Rawson wasn't finished yet. Just when we thought it was all over, his pellet was intercepted by another fine Crucian

Carp. He made no mistake with the net and then called out to say that it was bigger than the first one – and he was right! The super fish weighed 3lb 5oz and his aspirations had now been well and truly fulfilled – bravo that man!

Crucian triumph! - Rawson beams
as he cradles his specimen

BEYOND THE REEDS

9 5

Chapter VIII

Death on the Beach - 20ᵗʰ November 1976

The Cod were showing along the east coast, which was the signal for Richard Fobbester and myself to dust off the sea tackle and head towards Great Yarmouth. Our destination was actually Caister Beach where we were to meet Richard's dad who lived close by and had arranged our bait. The strategy was to fish the afternoon tide into the dark hours for the last of the flood before making the 130-mile journey home again. The bait consisted of Lugworms and fresh Herring that could be used either separately or as a cocktail if a larger bait was required. In an ideal world we would have preferred some Squid as back-up to the worms but, as they say, 'you can't always have your cake and eat it too!' Standard beachcasting rods and Mitchell Multiplying reels loaded with 18lb breaking strain line were the means to cast the 6oz breakaway leads past the third wave and hopefully beyond. The winds were light although it was bitterly cold and I was glad that I'd brought my trusty old WWII flying jacket along with the rest of the thermal togs. Anyway, we were all set up and ready to fish by 2pm, along with a score of other optimistic anglers who were positioned at intervals throughout the beach as the tide began to flood – Codding was certainly a popular pastime along the east coast.

Within minutes the traditional bells pegged onto both of our rods were jangling simultaneously and we reeled in a pair of Dabs which were probably too small for eating but they went into the bag all the same. Richard's dad, who used to run a fish and chip shop, was a handyman with a filleting knife and we hoped that he would be able to get at least a small amount of flesh from the little flatfish. More Dabs came ashore during the next hour or so and in fact it became difficult to avoid them. Even short casts of about 30 yards were still producing rattling bites from these voracious fish which all seemed to be of similar size, probably less than 8ozs. No Codling had shown as far as we could see from anywhere along the beach but it was still good sport in the Arctic conditions. It was just getting dark when Richard pointed out a disturbance on the surface of the sea some 30 or 40 yards from shore. We had never seen anything quite like that before from a shingle beach and, on closer inspection of this strange occurrence, the back and dorsal fin of a fish were clearly visible as it cut through the surf. We were transfixed as we followed the path of what we thought could only be a predator and a big one at that. The next thing we knew, the dorsal fin was heading straight towards us at a rate of knots that was difficult to comprehend. The wake caused by the fish's powerful movement was plain to see even in the rough surf close to the shoreline. We were standing in amazement when, suddenly, the fish thrust itself up onto the beach in a blaze of silver and white water. It was a beautiful Bream in magnificent condition that would have weighed upwards of 5lbs. Our immediate reaction was to rescue the beast and, to this end, it was hurled back into the sea where, to our relief, it took off strongly into the open sea. Once again we could follow the wake of the fish as it travelled at speed through the turbulent water, weaving and turning menacingly like a small Shark. It more or less disappeared from view and then changed course and headed for the shore again, seemingly with suicide in mind. The power of the fish was impressive and the momentum sent it up onto the shingle for a second time 50 yards to our right. Like a pair of fools we ran to its aid again and duly threw it back into the sea where, as before, it sped off into the open water. Yes, you can guess, five minutes later it was high and dry, apparently satisfied to be out of the sea. I suppose that we followed the doomed fish for about 45 minutes along the beach before giving it up as a bad job – the fish couldn't be saved.

Rays Bream

By the time we had made our way back to the rods, the place had fallen into complete darkness. The only light detectable was that radiating from the anglers' hurricane lanterns which twinkled into the distance like a dimly-lit Dickensian Street. It was time for the Cod and our focus was heightened for a while but it soon slipped back into a relaxed mode when it became obvious that the Cod shoals were absent. Our catches began to include some welcome Whiting, although they were also undersized and were returned to the sea. These fish seemed to prefer strips of Herring rather than the Lugworms that had taken the vast majority of the Dabs. The story of the unfortunate Bream was related to a passing angler returning home who advised us that the fish would have been a Rays Bream. Apparently these fish become disorientated and venture too far away from the warmer seas where they are happiest. Furthermore, it's not uncommon for them to commit suicide rather than remain in the cold water along this particular coastline. He also said that they made fine eating and hurried away to look for it before someone else capitalised on the find. Richard and I looked at each other, both knowing what a pair of clots we had been. The fish was beyond salvation and yet we had spurned our good fortune by throwing it back into the sea and consequently prolonging the poor fish's agony. It would have been a gastronomic delight for both of our families but now they had to rely on Richard's dad to salvage some flesh from our undersized Dabs – bon appetit!

*   *   *   *   *

Chapter IX

The Andy Mundy Memorial Pike Cup - 1st March 2009

Since hearing about this event, which commemorates the late Andy Mundy, I have had it in my mind, not surprisingly, to write a brief account about it. So, here goes...

You will probably recall that Andy was an avid and very successful specimen hunter who sadly lost his life in a boating accident at Queensford Lagoon in 1991. The commemorative event continues to be supported by both family and Andy's old fishing chums who always look forward to the annual get-together and a chance to get their hands on the prestigious cup. Whilst the competition is hotly contested by some very accomplished anglers, including the likes of Bob Jones of Redmire fame, it's obvious from those involved that the real enjoyment is in the partaking. Andy's brother Paul is the driving force behind the match which, incidentally, is to catch the largest Pike. Paul, who also takes part in the contest, has continued to ensure that the event takes place and that things run smoothly on the day. It is to be noted that each competitor is expected to make a donation for the pleasure of entering the contest, with the proceeds going into the coffers of the A.C.A. This match is normally held during the month of February but this year (2009) it had to be postponed until March because the lake was frozen over. Well, Rawson and I were honoured to be able to observe the entertainment at first hand, including the closing speeches and the presentation of the trophy to the winning angler by Paul and Andy's mother. I must say that I relished our stroll around the lake as it gave us a chance to chat to the competitors who were both approachable and refreshingly open. During our little ramble it soon occurred to me that the fishery was becoming more captivating with every visit. The flora and fauna were developing nicely and, as far as I could see, the place was now a veritable nature reserve. In fact, Paul had recently spotted a Water Rail skulking in the margins and he also showed me a picture of a rare Lizard that was sunning itself on one of his new 'Tench' platforms. I would have included the picture here but unfortunately the image had been taken on his mobile phone and wasn't quite sharp enough. Yes, I began to appreciate the enormity of Paul's achievement in producing a lasting legacy for his brother. The lake project has taken years of hard work and commitment but has paid off in a big way – take a bow, mate!

Anyway, I was surprised to find that the pegs I had thought would have produced the clonkers hadn't shown up any fish at all – so much for my reading of a water! In fact the captures seemed to be evenly spread around the fishery, which in a way was better than having one peg yielding numbers of fish because it helped to keep the suspense of the contest alive for longer. The weather had been kind and although the Pike hadn't played ball throughout the match, only providing sporadic sport, several good fish were caught, topped by an 18lb 8oz example that took the cup. I didn't actually get a photograph of the big one so, as you can see, I've taken the liberty of inserting an alternative showing a fish I caught at the lake a couple of months earlier!

MEMORIAL PIKE CUP

Lake No 13, "Andy's Lake"
Cotswold Water Park
South Cerney
CIRENCESTER

SUNDAY 15Th FEBRUARY 2009

Draw at 8.30 am

Fishing as from 9.00 am to 3.00 pm

All entries asked to make a donation, all of which will go to the A.C.A.

Any livebaits used to be taken from the water only

Andy's mother will present the cup to the captor of the largest pike

For further details contact Sandy Harris on
Cirencester 01285 641264 (evenings)

My Pike - 18lb 5ozs

Chapter X

Beyond The Reeds - 25th to 29th May 1984

For years my pal Richard Fobbester had been trying to persuade me to accompany him on a fishing trip to Ireland. He told me all about the 'craic' and I really didn't need any coaxing, but the problem was getting permission from my better half. Her reticence was quite understandable as she wasn't overly keen for me to leave our young family for the best part of a week to go on a fishing jolly. However, in 1984, it was finally agreed that I could go and, oh boy, what an initiation it turned out to be!

As always, Richard and I had planned the trip down to the nth degree and to this end we had ascertained that our best bet was to fish the River Shannon at Lanesborough in County Longford. Apparently, each year during the spring huge shoals of Bream migrate up the Shannon from Lough Ree to spawn in the waters just below the power station that is situated there. The fish are drawn to the warm water that is discharged continually into the river, having passed through the station's cooling systems. After spawning, the Bream remain in the river for a couple of weeks to recondition themselves before returning to the lough, so the timing of our visit was critical. In general terms, Lough Ree is 15 miles long and four miles wide and covers nearly 26,000 acres so one can only imagine how many Bream we could be talking about here. By good fortune, during our planning process Richard managed to obtain some local information on exactly where to fish through Jack Simpson, the tackle dealer (Simpson's of Turnford). This little acquisition, which included maps and diagrams of both the hot-water stretch and also some alternative pegs should a contingency plan be necessary, was pure gold dust! We had decided that our best ploy was to 'bivvy up' on the bank for the duration of our stay and fish solidly through four nights, which was the only time the Bream were active. According to our insider gen, the Bream were rarely caught during the daylight hours. The only problem that we could foresee in all this was having enough time to familiarise ourselves with the landscape and organise our equipment before it got dark on the first night. The timing of our ferry crossing from Holyhead to Dun Laoghaire meant that we could only have a few hours available to cover the 100-mile journey to Lanesborough. Frustratingly, an extra hour would have left us with ample time but, as it stood, it was in the balance whether we would make it.

As you can imagine, Richard's XR3i was loaded up to the hilt with our kit when we disembarked from the ferry on our arrival in the Emerald Isle. It was imperative that we got on our way in quick time but, sadly, we found ourselves at the back of the queue and headway was frustratingly slow. We seemed to take an age just getting out of the port itself, after which we had to contend with the traffic through Dublin, which wasn't much better. Luckily we had a high performance vehicle that would help us make up for lost time but for the moment it was bumper to bumper. Gradually the roads did become clearer the further we progressed but it was still going to be a close call whether we made it in time. I would have liked to be able to sit back and enjoy the ride as there was plenty to see along our route through Mullingar and Longford in the Midlands region. However, in view of the high speeds that we were travelling my eyes were firmly fixed on the road. In fact my heart was in my mouth during the last 20 miles or so when Richard was driving excessively fast along the very straight, very empty and yet very narrow roads. It was actually 11pm when we pulled in to Lanesborough Town but, amazingly, there was still adequate light for us to go about our business. I had been sceptical when Richard had told me that we could expect night to fall about an hour later than in England but, as always, he was right. Using our little map we soon found our way to the prime spots on the hot-water stretch and, surprisingly, they were devoid of anglers. The place had been given a fair amount of publicity and we thought that we would have to compete for space but in point of fact we had the stretch to ourselves! This turn of events should have set the alarm bells ringing but we were far to focused on other things to have considered anything being wrong. Our first priority was to start fishing rather than muck about organising the stores and sleeping quarters so most of our stuff was left in the car – we could deal with that in the morning. We had built up an idea in our minds of how things would be when we arrived but in reality they were somewhat different. The actual hot-water stretch, compared to the main river section on the other side of the dividing reed bed, was much narrower than we had been expecting – it was hard to imagine huge Bream hauls being caught from such a relatively small part of the river. One further observation was the seemingly low water levels which I felt would make the fishing easier for us.

We chose to start with our quiver tip rods fitted with betalites rather than utilise our alternative outfits with optonic alarms and bobbins, although we intended to keep our options open. Some groundbait was introduced into our chosen pitches, about 15 yards apart, and we were soon making our first casts into the relatively shallow water that I would estimate was between three and four feet deep. Alternating between Sweetcorn and Brandling Worms, we did start to catch a few Roach and Skimmers but it soon became alarmingly obvious that the Bream shoals had already departed – we had missed the boat! Stone the crows, this was a gigantic blow which for all intents and purposes meant that all our plans were now dead in the water. Our despondency was immediate and, in our tired state, we found it difficult to come to terms with the dilemma. We concluded that the Bream must have already completed their spawning activities and were probably on their way back to Lough Ree! It was back to the drawing board.

Richard hurriedly delved into his pocket and brought out the vital piece of paper showing the layout of the place and the alternative pegs. Using torchlight we got our bearings as best we could in the dark and ascertained that there was a small grassy peninsula on the other side of the river where we could try our luck. The diagram, which was very specific, showed that the fish were just 'beyond the reeds' that separated the hot-water stretch from the main river (refer to my own diagram on the opposite page which replicates the original). It was a difficult decision for us to move from the highly-prized pegs that we had looked forward to fishing for so long but at the same time it was a chance that we had to take – in truth we felt that our fishing holiday was over before it had begun. Anyway, we were fit to drop by the time we had carried our fishing equipment across Lanesborough's road bridge to the small grassy bank, but the good news was that it appeared we could park the car there too. This was a huge plus as it would give us a better sense of security and save us a whole lot of grief transporting our significant load.

The riverbed was very rocky and it took a lot of effort finding places to insert our rod rests in the dark. As it turned out, I wasn't particularly happy with my rather unstable set-up but decided to make do for the few hours that remained before dawn – I would endeavour to make a better job before the next night's session began. There was now a much wider expanse of river in which to cast and we had to make a judgement as to where the target area was before balling in some groundbait. The circumstances had changed and so did our choice of tackle. We now opted for our Specialist Bream rods and the optonic alarms rather than using the quiver rods as the feeling was that it was going to be more of a waiting game. Our end tackle comprised of a link-leger arrangement including an 18-inch

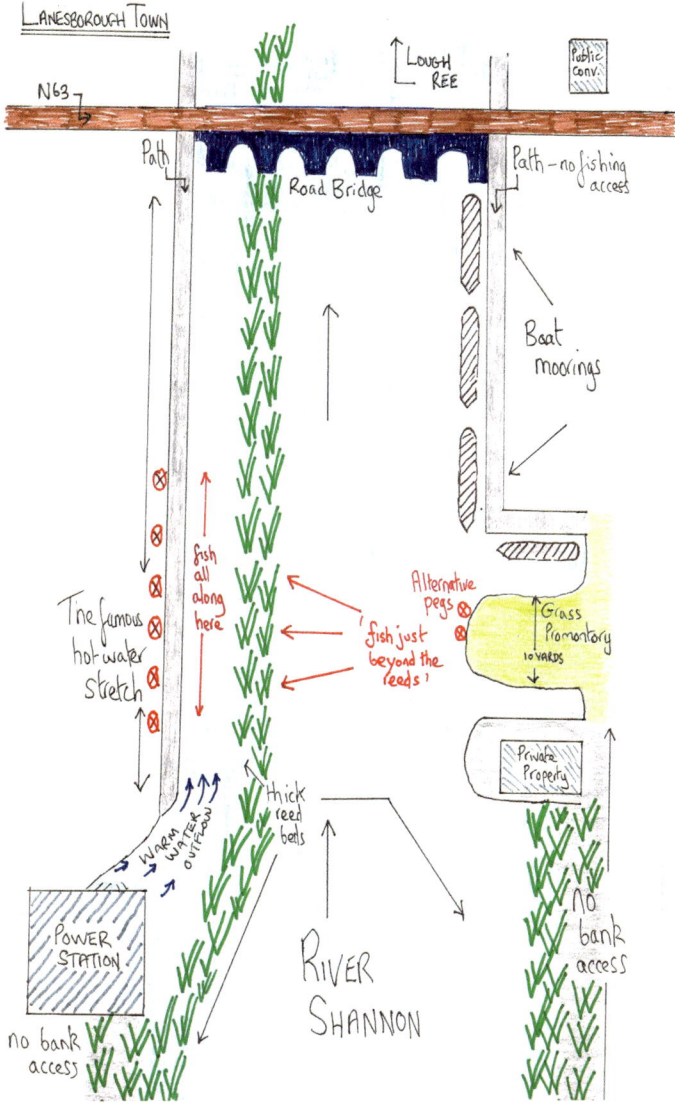

LANESBOROUGH TOWN

N63

Path

Road Bridge

LOUGH
REE

Public
conv.

Path – no fishing
access

Boat
moorings

The famous
hot-water
stretch

fish
all
along
here

Alternative
pegs

'fish just
beyond the
reeds'

Grass
Promontory
10 YARDS

Private
Property

WARM WATER
OUTFLOW

thick
reed
beds

POWER
STATION

no bank
access

RIVER
SHANNON

no
bank
access

hook link on which a size 10 Drennan specimen hook was tied. Main line was 6lb breaking strain Maxima fitted straight through. After a brief confab we decided to go for the famous 'Egan Octopus' for bait which was also described in our brief. It consisted of a number of Brandling Worms, each hooked once through the middle to form a wriggly bundle resembling a miniature Octopus. Apparently, Mr Egan was one of the local experts who had made some amazing catches using this bait. To compensate for the distance that we were casting and the flow of the river, our bobbins needed some added Swan shot to balance the set-up before we were ready to make our first casts. At last we thought we could sit back and relax for a while but it turned out we had hardly taken the weight off our feet when my optonic began to bleep. I waited for the bobbin to climb more or less to the butt ring before striking and connecting with something a lot more potent than I had been expecting. My first thoughts were that it was a big Tench because, as it neared shore, the water was boiling as the fish bored and struggled for freedom. In fact, I had to continually concede the 6lb line otherwise it would have surely snapped. I would certainly have bet my bottom dollar on it not being a Bream but in the event I would have lost my money – a lovely Bream surfaced in Richard's torch beam before he slipped the net under it. Wow, the fish was a new personal best, weighing in at 6lb 2oz, and my earlier gloom suddenly turned to elation. I couldn't believe the fight that it had given me – it battled like a demon all the way in and didn't give up the struggle quickly which was the usual Bream behaviour. I placed the fish in the keepnet and sat down just as Richard's optonic sounded off. Blimey, by the look of the bend in the rod another Slab was on the way to the net. The number, size and quality of these Bream were phenomenal and I was now glad that we had brought the vast amount of groundbait and hempseed that Richard had insisted upon. After a few more fish we both stepped up to size 6 hooks and increased the size of the 'Octopus'!

The sport continued throughout the night but stopped suddenly as if someone had switched off a light switch when that ethereal mist stage of dawn came upon us. In the relatively short period I had landed nine Bream with the largest weighing 7lb 12ozs and the smallest a tad under 4lbs, with a total weight in excess of 50lbs. Bream of this stature were as rare as rocking horse dung in England at the time and we couldn't believe our good fortune. All through the night it seemed like one of us was either playing a fish, which normally took several minutes, or weighing them for our fishing registers – talk about hectic! Richard's catch was similar to my own so overall we had accumulated over 100lbs of Bream. It had been a great night's fishing but by now we were in desperate need of sleep – I was actually beginning to hallucinate! Richard went off to fetch the car before we set up the sleeping quarters in one of the bivvies – the rest could wait 'til later.

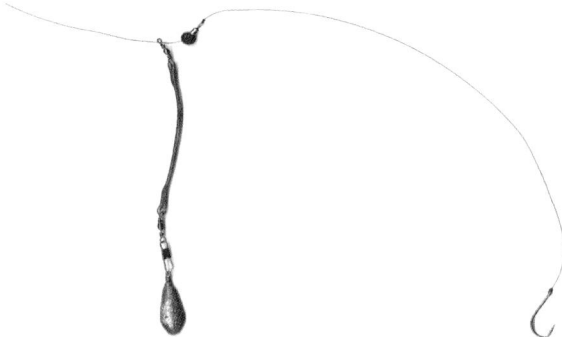

We crashed out completely for about six hours before a friendly old Irish fellow woke us up to enquire if he could fish with us. We told him to go right ahead and he sat down between our rods and cast a huge float into the flow. He looked a picture in his chequered shirt, tie and waistcoat and an ill-fitting suit that looked as though he'd slept in it – great stuff. It must have taken us a couple of hours to get organised before we were ready to film our catch and release the fish. Our new Irish friend helped us with the task and I used my cine camera to record the event with the sounds of Bob Marley's 'Legend' album playing in the background on Richard's 'Brixton briefcase'! The film sequence attracted a few extra onlookers, including a German visitor who also latched himself onto us. His English wasn't too good, our German was non-existent and we had quite a laugh trying to communicate some of the finer points of our methods to him. Our new comrades joined us for some egg and bacon rolls that we rustled up bankside and, all in all, our little international conference was quite a success. It was gratifying to know that all our equipment had been fully organised, including the second bivvy containing all our provisions and spare tackle. The worm supply had been stored safely away in a cool place and a large bin full of hempseed that would last us for the duration was left to soak – we were ready for the ensuing session.

The hunger pangs began in earnest during the early evening and we decided to take a walk into town. I was a bit reluctant to leave all our kit behind unattended but Richard, the old hand, assured me that it would be safe. He explained that he'd never experienced any problems in Ireland before and it was just the normal thing to do at that time – my faith in human nature was suddenly reinforced and I was beginning to fall in love with this place! We soon found a bar and I can still remember my first pint of Irish stout. I was fascinated with its preparation alone, which must have taken the best part of five minutes to complete.

It was mesmerising to see the brew's bubbles working up towards the head before the barman levelled it off skilfully and added the final topping – marvellous! The taste was exquisite and for some reason it was so much better than the stuff served up in England. In fact I was so taken with it that I actually wrote a rhyme describing the pouring process, which was included in my first publication 'The Angling Bug' under the title 'Callans O' the Bridge'. After my Guinness initiation we ordered some Irish stew which also hit the spot in every way, before returning to our temporary abode on the river.

It wasn't yet dark but we still cast the rods out just in case the Bream were on the prowl. Plenty of groundbait laced with hempseed followed but the Bream shoals either hadn't arrived or weren't playing ball yet. Boat traffic throughout the day was brisk but I must say that I was saddened to see a pleasure launch go by with a score of dead Pike hanging high over the decks for everyone to see. The German crew seemed to be cock-a-hoop with their catch which had been taken from Lough Ree. The slaughter of these fish for trophies may have been abhorrent to us but I believe it was just normal tradition for many of the foreign anglers at that time – hopefully circumstances are different nowadays. Anyway, we were singing along to Bob Marley's rendition of 'Is this Love' when my indicator twitched skywards and I struck into an Eel which resulted in the need to tie a fresh hook link – Eels weren't in the game plan and I hoped that no more of them were going to come our way. Fortunately they didn't but we did catch a few Roach, Rudd, Perch and a solitary Jack Pike before darkness descended and the Bream began to feed. Richard was the first to feel that satisfying heavy thumping of another Slab at the end of the line just as track five 'Buffalo Soldier' was filling the airwaves. It weighed 5lb 12ozs and he nonchalantly put it in the net without so much as a comment – blimey, talk about complacency. The fish were special all right but at this prolific venue they were becoming just run-of-the-mill as time went on. Our second night of sport continued as before but perhaps not quite up to the same impetus. We finished up with a very satisfying 80lb bag which included a fair number of six-pounders and one seven that Richard took.

The third night turned out to be the most productive of our four sessions, resulting in a mammoth bag of Bream which was well over 200lbs! The fish probably fed in earnest because of the warm and wet conditions that prevailed. There wasn't a whisper of wind and the drizzly rain that had a tendency to saturate everything in its path very quickly was in the air for most of the night. My particular catch included three more seven-pounders, six more six-pounders and a stack of four and fives. I didn't have the inclination to note down Richard's catch details at the time but he fared similarly and by morning we were not only shattered when we fell into our beds but probably a bit smelly too! As you know, Bream slime is fearful stuff that tends to get everywhere and so by now we were definitely in need of a shower which, in our circumstances, was an impossibility. However, despite the grime and the sleep deprivation we couldn't have been more content as we drifted off into the Land of Nod that morning.

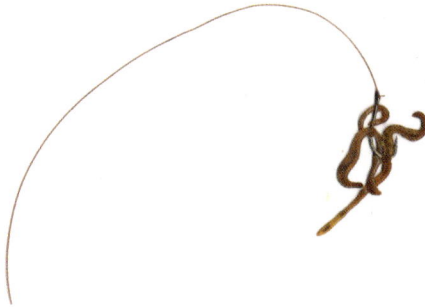

A high percentage of the fish that we had caught had a 'two
-tone' appearance that I hadn't come across previously.
This strange phenomenon has been the subject of much
debate over the years but, as far as I can make out, there
have been no definitive conclusions made. I don't have any
theories about it myself other than saying that the fish we
encountered were in prime condition and certainly showed
no signs of ill-health, which is contrary to some opinions.
There is no mistaking a 'two-tone' Bream when you catch
one. It is as if a dividing line has been drawn vertically
down the fish's flank from dorsal fin to gut. One side of the
line has a light shade and the other a dark one. I'll be
surprised if there hasn't been a scientific explanation or
diagnosis for this peculiarity but, having trawled the
internet, I have been unable to find anything conclusive
myself.

"Two-tone Bream"

Yet again, our final night produced the goods with an average yield of well over 100lbs of fish between us. It was fitting that my last Bream, which weighed 7lb 1oz, was the only fish caught in daylight and therefore was the only battle sequence captured on film. Perhaps saying daylight was a bit of an exaggeration: it was actually the half-light stage just as the sun had peeped above the horizon, but what the hell. Richard had a couple more sevens and there were another dozen or so six-plussers in our bag when we came to film them. It had been a wonderful fishing experience and my only regret was not having brought a 'stills' camera along to record some of the memories. Other than ten minutes of stimulating home movie action, which was great to look back on, I don't have any photographic records as such of the trip. I've therefore had to rely on Richard for the photographs contained in this story. Anyway, as soon as the fishing was over there was no time for us to sleep as we had a ferry to catch. It was a case of decamping quickly and getting on the road to Dublin where, time permitting, we hoped to finish off the holiday in style with a full Irish breakfast. Before we departed though, it was imperative that some personal hygiene was employed, for obvious reasons. We had been living like a pair of vagrants for the best part of a week and I was quite sure that third parties would have been all too aware of the fact. We had been fortunate to be able to take advantage of the one cold tap in the local public convenience, where we endeavoured to maintain a daily semblance of cleanliness, although you can appreciate that this did have its limitations. You will also understand that before heading home it was necessary for us to make a final early morning visit to our 'wash room' for one last wash and brush-up. In the event there wasn't anyone around so we decided to go the whole hog and strip off to our birthday suits ready for a thorough scrub down instead of the cursory 'splash and run'. It turned out to be a painful ordeal and I'm sure our shrieks of agony could be heard from far afield as the freezing cold water came into contact with the tender bits! As luck would have it, we were going through the torture when a chap came in, took one look, laughed and walked out again! What he must have thought was anyone's guess but we still chuckle about the dent today.

Our first Irish mission was one that I shall never forget and our success was all down to that little piece of paper that Richard chanced upon in his local tackle shop. Without it we would never have known about the little grass-covered peninsula on the opposite bank that turned out to be so fruitful for us. During our four-night campaign we had taken well over 500lbs of quality Bream between us and all from a spot marked on the sketch as 'just beyond the reeds'!

An upstream view of the mighty River Shannon at
Lanesborough from the little grassy knoll.

For the record, Richard returned to the very same spot at
Lanesborough the following year with Dave Wilson and,
during their campaign, they accumulated a massive Bream
haul of 865lbs! Richard took the biggest Bream of the four-
day visit, which went 8lb 9ozs and was the only eight-
pounder caught. Dave landed several sevens, one of which
is shown in the picture below which was published in the
Angling Times in June 1985.

Angling Times, Wednesday, June 19, 1985

Irish bream

● HERTFORDSHIRE angler
Dave Wilson sampled a great
taste of Irish bream when he
and friend Richard Foddester
took a total of 865 lb during a
four-day holiday on the River
Shannon at Lansborough, Ireland.

Chapter XI

Salt-Water Titbits

The sea acts like a magnet to me for some reason and I can only conclude that I must have a seafaring connection somewhere in my ancestral past. Yes, I do fancy the idea that some of my forefathers may have been associated with the sea in some way. It would be nice to think that my maritime blood line could have included a romantic individual such as a smuggler or a pirate, or even an ale-drenched Old Salt spinning yarns in a far-away quayside tavern. I am certainly very much at home when I am on the coast where I can sit for hours looking at the ever-changing view of a seascape. It has also provided me with some diverse challenges and some great memories, although there have been some hair-raising moments as well. I've been out at sea on a couple of occasions when a sudden squall has cropped up and fishing has become nigh on impossible. These incidents have usually ended up with the crew just hanging on as the boat has pitched heavily in the swell, with most of the anglers succumbing to sickness and even rolling on the decks – one never forgets those times! Perhaps the worst experience I've endured was when I was foolhardily fishing from exposed rocks on the Cornish coast during storm force winds. I was under the false impression that I was safe perched on my high vantage point, but a freak wave broke over the rock and I was engulfed. My feet were swept from under me and it was only by locking my elbows into a crevice that I was saved from taking a long drop into a raging sea, and certain death. I actually laughed about it at the time but I still have nightmares about the incident. I must say that I now take a greater interest in the prevailing conditions as it has finally sunk into my thick skull that the sea can be a dangerous beast and should be treated with the utmost respect – and not before time, you daft old twerp! In saying that however, fishing in the sea is still great fun and can be very rewarding for at least nine months of the year. There are so many different species to go for, requiring a whole range of tactics to catch them, and the challenges are far-reaching. For a flavour of some further escapades, please read on:

Rod Rattlers Of The Dart -
1st November 2008

Taking a rod along on our latest jaunt to Dartmouth was a last-minute decision and one that I'm glad I made. My reticence had been because there was only going to be very limited time available and, more importantly, I was doubtful whether the summer species would still be in the estuary. In order to get a better handle of the situation, I checked my fishing diary and was surprised to discover that I'd caught a whole raft of species during the corresponding week the year before. It seemed very late in the season to have caught these fish but it did provide a glimmer of hope and I wasn't about to waste it. Without further ado I gathered together the usual light tackle outfit and raided the deep freeze for some bait. Consulting the tide table, it looked like there was only going to be one suitable time to fish during our short stay, which happened to be after dark. This one chance to fish was all that I needed so the speculative session was pencilled into our social calendar!

A chill ran through me like a knife cutting through butter as I made my way along the quay towards the old cannon – I'm sure I never used to feel the cold as much as this, it must be a sign of old age. There was a fresh north-easterly wind blowing and sleet was in the air when I assembled the quiver tip rod and fixed spool reel loaded with 6lb breaking strain line. The weather was hardly conducive to fishing for summer species and deep down I was already preparing myself for failure. Furthermore, there were no other anglers on site which was another ominous sign that things could be difficult. The night was a dark one but the old Victorian lamppost sited at the end of the esplanade would provide enough illumination for baiting up and also allow me to register any bites – if I should be so lucky that is! The session began one hour before the peak of high tide and my intention was to fish for one hour into the ebb, giving me a couple of hours of the best fishing time. A section of raw King Prawn was impaled on a size 8 hook before the fixed paternoster rig with a mere 1oz lead was lowered down the side of the quay wall to the sea floor. It was important to tighten the line to the lead quickly to ensure that the bait wafted above bottom, thus hopefully avoiding a Crab attack. Response to the bait at this particular spot was normally instantaneous so I was more than a little concerned when after five minutes or so there hadn't been so much as a nibble. I had actually resigned myself to the fact that the Ballans and Corkwings had already departed for their winter haunts and the place was now devoid of fish life. It looked like I'd drawn a blank but, amazingly, as I reached out for the rod ready to leave for the nearest tavern, the tip pulled around as a fish hooked itself, taking the bait. The fish was reeled up and brought over the balustrade but its elongated shape was not what I had been expecting and I was puzzled as to what I'd caught. I brought it to hand before holding it aloft into the light from the street lamp and was thrilled with the revelation – a new species! This was confirmed by its colouring and three barbels, two of which appeared on the snout and one on the chin. It was a Shore Rockling and the gamble to fish had paid dividends. I'd previously caught a number of Three Bearded Rockling, which are very similar to their 'Shore' cousins, but there is one telling difference. The former fish have a reddish-brown mottled appearance, whereas Shore Rockling have a uniform dull colouring. I always like to get a photograph of my PBs but cursed to myself when I realised that I hadn't brought the camera with me – scatterbrain!

Whilst the summer species had gone it was evident that the winter species had arrived and I had to step up both hook and bait size and change tactics to capitalise. Instead of dropping the rig down the side of the quay, I cast out about 30 yards into deeper water and the change was dramatic. No sooner had the bait settled than the rod tip was pounding and the action continued non-stop for the duration. All in all I must have banked about 30 more fish, consisting of Whiting and Poor Cod in equal quantities, before the bait supply ran out. Poor Cod are very similar to Pouting but can be distinguished by their shiny, coppery appearance and an outlandishly large eye. They are by no means a rare fish but, in saying that, they don't often fall to my rods. I have caught them previously off Aberystwyth some years ago, but have seen little of them since. Poor Cod don't grow to mammoth proportions; in fact the rod-caught record stands at only 11ozs according to my latest list. They may have been on the small side but, oh boy, talk about taking the bait with aggression! These little demons sent the tip flying around in what I can only compare to typical Barbel takes – no kidding. The resultant strikes would inevitably meet with no resistance at all but more often than not there would be a small Poor Cod attached on recovery of the rig! The Whiting were a different kettle of fish though – excuse the pun. These toothy critters were much larger and needed careful attention as they were winched up from the sea. Many of them were big enough to eat and my wife wasn't too impressed when I told her that I'd released them all. I did volunteer to try again on the morning tide but for some reason she seemed to become even more animated at this suggestion! Whilst I knew the Whiting shoals were around, I hadn't expected them to venture into the River Dart itself, especially in such numbers. They must have been thick on the ground because in most instances the bites occurred before I'd had time to tighten the line.

Anyway, this little bonanza had been a total surprise to me, which is so typical of how fishing can be sometimes. It is this unpredictability, mixed with a modicum of suspense of course, that makes fishing so appealing to me. Things rarely go strictly according to plan and I have now conditioned myself to always expect the unexpected. Looking back at the night's events, the quiver tip rod and light tackle had been great fun but at the same time were totally inadequate for that type of fishing. Next time I shall make sure that I am better equipped, when perhaps I will be lucky enough to encounter some Codling as well...

Prisk Cove – 18th May 2009

My attention was suddenly drawn to the television one evening when the emphasis turned from farming to rock pool rambling. I couldn't believe my eyes when I saw a fish that is virtually unknown being caught from a beach in the Helford River region on Cornwall's Lizard peninsula. The BBC had sent a film crew armed with buckets and nets to produce a clip on the secret world of rock pools as part of their Nature's Calendar programme. The unusual fish in question was the Cornish Suckerfish, which is also known as the Shore Clingfish (Lepadogaster lepadogaster). Being an annual visitor to The Lizard I decided to try and find out exactly where these fish had been filmed. The internet was obviously the first vehicle to begin the investigation and it didn't take long for me to discover the location of Prisk Cove, which lies just south of Rosemullion Head. Consequently, the new target was put onto my agenda.

Cornish Suckerfish/Clingfish
(photograph courtesy of Carol Tucker)

My timing could have been a little better when I ventured along the coastal path towards this rather isolated cove, as the tide had only been ebbing for an hour or so. Arriving early meant that there were very few rock pools available to seek out these relatively rare fish but fortunately I had brought my MK1 Dangler special which was a big advantage. This little telescopic rod allows me to place baits precisely into cracks and crevices in depths of up to several feet. I had also brought along some Shellfish and Squid for bait that I hoped would be irresistible to the Suckerfish, although this tactic was only guesswork. First stop was a lovely L-shaped pool which contained an array of sea life including Dog Whelks, Shore Crabs and plenty of seaweed, although it transpired that there were very few nooks and crannies to try my luck. Not surprisingly, there were no takers in the first spot but the second looked like a much better prospect. It was a little deeper and the boulders on the bottom were the perfect place to present a bait. Keeping a low profile, I carefully lowered a section of Prawn on a size 16 into a small gap between two rocks which appeared to have some nice cavities beneath them. Almost immediately, a fish shot out from its rocky sanctuary, sucked in the bait and then disappeared under the boulders again, all in a fraction of a second. I struck and pulled up a fish which was unexpectedly hefty for such a diminutive pool at the top of the beach. It was certainly a Goby but of which variety I was unsure – a photograph was taken so I could identify it at a later date. It was interesting to see that the pelvic fins on its underside were fused into a circular shaped suction cup, however this fish wasn't the one I'd been hoping for. The next offering – a strip of Squid – was once again taken on the drop and I caught another belting Goby that was by far the largest I'd ever seen. This fish was enormous (by Gobiidae standards that is) and I kicked myself for not having brought along my precision scales to weigh the thing accurately. Anyway, during the next half hour I caught a whole lot more of them but, despite covering most of the middle shore, I didn't get a sniff of a Cornish Suckerfish. The hunt had been a lot of fun but to crack the target I would have to try some new tactics on another occasion.

This fish was later identified as a Rock Goby. It wasn't the big one, which was half as big again, I chose this shot because it shows the features of this species rather well.

The location of Prisk Cove is slightly off the beaten track so, just in case some of you get the opportunity to visit the area, the local directions have been detailed below:

Ordnance Survey Map Number 103 – The Lizard (Falmouth and Helston)

Map Reference: SW795276

Start Point: Mawnan Church car park (map reference SW788275)

From the car park, walk to the right of the lychgate, passing over a high stile beside a wooden gate. Follow the footpath signposted to Durgan but turn left at the first opportunity. Zigzag your way down to the wooded valleyside, keeping to the obvious path. Climb up the wooden steps out of Mawnan Grebe, pass above Shag Rock, looking ahead to see large ships moored just off Falmouth. Now, about ten minutes into the walk, look across Falmouth Bay to a small white lighthouse at St Anthony on the Roseland. Cross a wooden stile into a field and follow the path above Prisk Cove into the adjoining field. After about 40 yards, turn sharp right into the small access track down to the beach. Journey time: approximately 20 minutes.

Porthleven, Cornwall – 21st May 2009

Having arrived at our holiday accommodation in the heart of Porthleven Town, my first objective was to book a boat fishing trip on 'Danda', skippered by Stuart Athay. I've used Stuart's expertise on previous occasions and, in my opinion, there is no better person in the charter angling game. In fact, the cover picture of my first fishing book – 'It Started with a Perch' – was actually taken on Danda in June 2004. However, the prospect of getting out this time didn't look at all good because the weather was awful, but Stuart did give us a shred of hope. The forecast for the week ahead predicted an easing of the winds on the following Thursday - six days hence – so, based on that information, I made a provisional booking for six of my family and friends. I was a bit concerned because, apart from Rawson, the rest of our crew were novices who might not appreciate a 'rough' initiation into the world of boat fishing. I could only hope that all would be well on the day but, either way, it was gratifying to know that they would be in capable hands. Stuart is the friendly, approachable type who always does his level best for his anglers. He has acquired his knowledge through angling from a young age, which blossomed when he decided that he would rather be out on the charter boat than sitting in his father's tackle shop. To cut a long story short, despite his young years he is now a very successful commercial fisherman who is well known throughout his local community.

As the week progressed our chances of a day at sea got better and I felt that it was about time for Stuart and I to have a chat. It transpired that his intention was to fish a reef mark which would give us some alternatives and hopefully ensure that the beginners caught some fish. Primarily, the idea was to fish for Pollack on jellyworm lures before changing over to feathers, which could be baited for Whiting or left unbaited for Mackerel. In the circumstances this was certainly a good plan but I enquired if there were any other species that I could fish for at the same mark. I went through some of the new sea species that are on my target list and Stuart said there were two possibilities. Firstly there was Haddock, although these fish only turn up randomly and the chances of catching one were very slim. The other was the Cuckoo Wrasse which he felt I had a good chance of connecting with on baited feathers – this was great news as I'd been after one of those for several years.

Early on Thursday morning we were greeted with the news that we all wanted to hear - Stuart had given us the green light to sail. However, at the same time, he did bring me back to earth with a word of caution: my Cuckoo Wrasse was largely dependent on catching a fresh Mackerel for bait, which was now in jeopardy. The atrocious weather had churned up the sea for a week, leaving it in a cloudy state that wasn't conducive to hauling Mackerel. It was an unknown quantity until we actually got out there, so I would just have to keep my fingers crossed and wait and see. At least the winds had abated somewhat and, in theory, the clarity should have improved, which would certainly help my cause. Anyway, we boarded 'Danda' at 11.45am outside the Ship Inn, and Stuart headed out to one of his favourite marks, at the back of the Welloe Rock. It was the first time we had seen the sun all week and it was nice to sit back and soak up the rays and enjoy the scenery during the steam. As we wended our way through the waves I was trying to pick out all the places along the coastline that we had become familiar with over the years. At the closest point, the tin mine at Rinsey Head and the golden sands at Praa were clearly recognisable. Scanning further afield brought into view the majestic St Michael's Mount situated in Mounts Bay, along with miles of shoreline stretching from Penzance, Newlyn and Mousehole around as far as Lamorna – what a spectacle!

When Stuart had reached his destination, he took time out to provide our newcomers with some on-the-job tuition on the use of rod and multiplying reel. They must have been quick learners because within minutes they were all reeling up the jelly worms from the reef like pro's, in search of the Pollack. In fact my son, Lee, got a 4lb fish on the first drop down and, as he was one of the novices, I felt the pressure lift slightly – only four more to go. Son-in-law Darren was the next to catch another eatable-sized Pollack, which meant that another novice had scored. Without going into details, everybody caught Pollack, apart from myself that is, and as you may have guessed the ribbing began in earnest. Anyway, in the meantime Stuart found a stray Mackerel and I now had some bait for the Cuckoos. Dispensing with the jellyworm rod, I changed over to one with feathers and I was told to bait the bottom two hooks. I was surprised to hear that a chunk of Mackerel was the best bait for a Cuckoo Wrasse as in the past I had always used Squid and shellfish – maybe that's where I had been going wrong! Stuart explained that I needed to bounce the lead across the bottom as we drifted or I would have no chance of connecting with a Cuckoo. It was a dangerous game because the lead was prone to getting jammed into the rocks, but there was no alternative as the prospect of catching one with the bait in mid-water was nil. He also said that I would probably get about 20 rattly bites before connecting with one of these elegant fish. This comment seemed a bit odd to me but I just had to see what happened in practice. It was a great feeling, knowing that at last I was actually fishing for a Cuckoo with the right bait and tackle and, more importantly, in a place where they were abundant.

The baited feathers were lowered to the bottom on the 20lb breaking strain braid and I gradually got into the rhythm of bumping the lead across the rough ground. As Stuart had predicted, the rattly bites came at regular intervals but every time I seemed to strike into fresh air. It was frustrating and I now understood exactly what he had meant by his earlier comment. However, after about ten minutes and 20 strikes, I did manage to connect with something. My pulse began to race in anticipation as I reeled up my first fish of the day which, surprisingly, turned out to be a Codling. This unplanned catch could just as easily have been a Haddock and what a turn-up for the book that would have been – talk about buzzing with excitement, I couldn't get a new bait back to the reef quick enough. The sea was a bit lumpy but fortunately none of us had been sick, which was another worry lifted from my shoulders. In fact, everything was going swimmingly. The fish box was gradually being filled with Pollack and even our lady aboard, Emma, was not only coping with the conditions admirably but also taking her share of the catch. Rawson's son, James, looked favourite to win the sweepstake kitty for the largest fish of the day – he had boated a lovely Pollack weighing about 6½lbs and it was looking like Stuart had come up trumps for us again. I was also heartened to see that everybody was returning the smaller fish to the sea after capture. There had been no directive to do this so it would appear that most people are now conscious of the need to conserve our fish stocks – that's the spirit! Anyhow, once again I found myself striking into thin air as the rattly bites occurred and then, out of the blue, the rod arched and my second fish was on the way up from the reef. Reeling steadily, I waited with bated breath for the fish to appear and - bingo! - I could see flashes of turquoise from a beautiful male Cuckoo Wrasse. It was brought safely to hand – not a big fish, perhaps 10ozs, but - oh boy! - was I a happy bunny. It was time for a little jig!

By the end of the day I had caught four Cuckoos: three male fish and one female, with the biggest fish going just over a pound. With the exception of the ultra-rare Baillon's Wrasse and the Scale Rayed Wrasse, which are not viable targets, I have now caught all the other species of Wrasse that exist in British waters. The question was what to do next. On the way back to port, Stuart and I discussed other possibilities and he felt the best bet was to take Danda to the Penzance area next time to try for a Greater Weever - roll on next year!

Fishing over rough ground at the back of the Welloe Rock

Male Cuckoo Wrasse

The challenge to catch a Weever is very appealing to me and I shall look forward to taking up Stuart's offer to try for one on my next visit to Cornwall. I know very little about these curious fish that are rarely targeted by anglers, apart from their fearsome reputation for stinging the unsuspecting with their poisonous spines. Meanwhile, it looks like I shall have to delve into the archives for the best tactics to catch them - the thrill of the chase begins again!

Chapter XII

Tacklin' Down

Another busy fishing period has come to an end but before I sign off there are a couple of subjects associated with the sport that I'd like to air.

Firstly, the floods of 2007. Living as I do in one of the worst affected flood areas in the country, you won't be surprised to learn that I have become somewhat sanitised to these events over the course of time. Disappearing fields, disappearing roads and detours at times of flood have become par for the course for people living in the general area of the River Severn between Worcester and Gloucester. However, whereas the problems used to be mainly restricted to the winter months, incidents of flooding are now becoming commonplace and can happen at any time. Furthermore, they appear to be more prolonged of late which I can only assume is due to the build-up of greenhouse gases in the atmosphere and the consequential phenomenon of global warming. The probability is that things aren't going to get any better so we can expect more of the same. The floods of 2007 were certainly the most severe that I have witnessed so far and these took place in the summer, which tends to support my theory. A point of concern is that prior to the 2007 event I don't remember there being a problem of fish losses through flooding, but now the situation appears to have changed. I have received disturbing reports from fellow anglers of vast numbers of Bream being found dead in the fields surrounding the River Severn below Worcester. These fish weren't only Skimmers either, with many approaching double figure weights. They have obviously perished after becoming stranded while seeking respite from a prolonged bout of spate conditions. To highlight the severity of this fish kill I would also point out that I haven't had a sniff of a Bream during an exhaustive

Barbel campaign since this tragedy. There is definitely something amiss here because previously these fish were always a continual nuisance, despite measures being taken to deter them such as the use of outsized baits. Of course my lack of success with the Bream could just be a coincidence but my instincts tell me otherwise. On a similar theme, it is also a little worrying that at the time of writing even the Barbel have not appeared in their usual numbers throughout the lower reaches of both the Severn and Avon. This too could be as a result of the severe floods of 2007 – only time will tell.

Moving southwards to the Tewkesbury area, one of my angling companions spent a whole day trying to save thousands of young fish which he'd discovered in a drainage ditch that was drying up after the floods had receded. He managed to transfer bucket loads of fish of varying types including Tenchlets back to the River Avon, but his efforts were a mere drop in the ocean compared to the number of fish remaining. It is also notable that Dave's desperate attempts to save these fish were carried out in one small accessible area so the whole extent of the problem can only be imagined. All in all, these dreadful floods were a disaster – not only were hundreds of people made homeless but there was also a catastrophic loss of fish life as never seen before. The natural replenishment of these local waterways could take several years to complete, if in fact they ever do return to anything like normality. This situation has not yet been fully appreciated and the galling part is that extensive building work has continued on the local flood plains since the events of 2007 which, in my view, beggars belief. Apparently one particular construction site curiously changed its name midway through the building process from 'The Water Meadows', which described the environment admirably, to nothing more than 'The Meadows'. Now this audacious and yet very clever ploy smacks of deceit to me and was more than likely done to avoid criticism and/or awkward enquiries. In my eyes, building in areas like this is sheer folly and can only compound problems for the future. I fail to understand how anyone with a quantum of logic can sanction such building programmes, unless perhaps there is some other ulterior motive of which we are unaware. The tragedy is that by the time things go sour and the flooding worsens because of these crass decisions to build, the bureaucrats will not be held to account. The consequences could be very serious indeed and I can't help feeling a sense of impotence as well as perceived injustice.

Tewkesbury town centre cut off during the 2007 floods

Secondly, memorabilia and collectibles. I thought I'd write a chapter on this subject as I'm sure that many of you who love the sport have collected a few mementos along the way to complement your passion. Apart from updating an ever-growing angling library, I am constantly on the look-out for bits and pieces of a fishy nature to display in my cabinets at home. Over the years I have gained much pleasure from looking around antique markets, junk shops and the like in search of anything old and appealing. The good news is that most of the objects are relatively small and can be stored easily. Unusual items are always welcomed and so I'll mention a couple of finds that some of you might find interesting. Not so long ago I came across an old mahogany 'fid' dating back to 1820 in a shop in the Cotswold village of Broadway. A fid is a small conical-shaped instrument that was used by mariners to repair sails and fishing nets. Ever since I acquired it the piece has become a topic of conversation with visitors and, not only that, it looks better with every polish! Another item that has some history is a 'Scrimshaw' thimble that I picked up for a few pence on my travels. 'Scrimshaw' was the name given to the artwork carried out by the Inuit and Whalemen during the early 1800's. They utilised the by-products of their trade such as the teeth of Sperm Whales and Walrus tusks by etching a design with the point of a knife or a sharpened sail needle. These etchings usually depicted a ship or a whaling scene and were brought brought to life when tobacco juice, candle black or Squid ink were rubbed into the carving – great stuff. Anyway, above all I love collecting old floats, lures, angling club badges and postage stamps showing different species of fish emanating from all over the world. These items add a bit of colour to the collection and help to bring back memories of the early days. Apart from the general run-of-the-mill angling paraphernalia, there are also a few specialities that I would like to describe in case anyone is interested in taking up the collecting challenge. These are as follows:

'*The Gallant Fishers*' by Royal Doulton. This wonderful series comprises of a whole range of items including rack plates, jugs of different shapes and sizes, ashtrays, loving cups and tobacco jars. These articles were first manufactured in 1906 although the date when they were withdrawn from the production line is unknown – my guess would be during the years of World War II. The scenes and titles are based upon that famous book 'The Compleat Angler' by Izaak Walton, published in 1653. Most of the items contain a distinctive 'willow tree' patterned border with the main subject being the profile of a fisherman that could be Izaak himself. There is also an evocative quotation embossed around the rim of each item that I'm sure will appeal to many who get a glimpse of this work. For a flavour of these old English extracts I have listed a few samples below:

'The jealous Trout that now did lie
Rose at a well dissembled fly'

'Perch or Pike, Roach or Dace
We do chase'

'Friend who is more welcome to my dish
Than to my angle was my fish'

'Oh the gallant fishers' life
It is the best of any'

'I care not to fish in the seas
Fresh rivers best my mind do please'

Gallant Fishers ware is by no means commonplace but can be found if one is persistent enough – in my view these pieces not only look attractive but are also a sound investment.

Annual Dartmouth Fishing Festival commemorative plates. I'm not too sure when production of these plates began but my earliest acquisition dates back to the 1963 festival. This particular year features a Wrasse although I believe a different species of fish is chosen for each occasion – it's that old species thing again! The plates are no more that six inches in diameter which means that they can be displayed without taking up too much space – always a collector's dilemma. I first clapped eyes on them in the George and Dragon pub in Dartmouth where they were displayed around the wall in the main bar – very impressive they were too. After a few enquiries, the landlord pointed me in the direction of Dartmouth Angling Club, situated close to the quay, where I discovered a whole lot more of these plates. For a signed book or two, I was given a few of their doubles to start my own collection and I've never looked back since.

Cynicus, Old Postcards and Watercolour Paintings. Cynicus was the pseudonym of an artist named Martin Anderson who was born in 1854 in Leuchars, Fife. He became famous for his satirical cartoons which were subsequently used to produce the designs of the first comic postcards. The Cynicus Publishing Company was launched in Tayport in 1902 and at first was a roaring success although the timing of the enterprise could not have been worse. Unfortunately the 'depression' years followed and the business ultimately folded in 1911. Whilst Cynicus was responsible for producing postcards with comical scenarios covering a range of subjects, there are about a dozen or so that are associated with fishing in particular. These make super little collectibles and can be tracked down without too much trouble or expense. The pièces de résistance however are the small watercolour paintings that were produced at the same time and depict the same subjects as those shown on the postcards. The original artwork can surprisingly still be found and normally retails for less than £50, which isn't bad for a piece more than a hundred years old. For the record I have listed below some fishing-based titles to look out for:

'St Machar' – a monk fishing

'The pleasures of hope' – a line of anglers with umbrellas

'Still fishing dearest and not a nibble' - I haven't come across this one yet so no description available

'Three fishers went trailing out into the wet' – self-explanatory

'I am dropping a line to see if I can get ...' - Dutch boy fishing

'Always getting something' – man catching a kettle

'Fishing for a young man' – lady on balcony fishing (Juliet)

'Water nymph' – mermaid appearing at the end of a monk's fishing line

'Three to bait a line' – three schoolboys sharing one rod.

Good hunting!

Cynicus watercolour painting and corresponding postcard